AF364201

Larisa Seklitova
Lyudmila Strelnikova

PEARLS
OF THE HIGHER TRUTHS

Encounters with the Higher Cosmic Consciousness

CosmUnity
2024

"PEARLS OF THE HIGHER TRUTHS". Encounters with the Higher Cosmic Consciousness / L. Seklitova, L. Strelnikova. – 1 edition in English. – CosmUnity, 2024. – 203 p.

Original version: "ЖЕМЧУЖИНЫ ВЫСШИХ ИСТИН". Контакты с Высшим Космическим Разумом. / Л. А. Секлитова, Л. Л. Стрельникова. – 12 editions, 2007–2022. – M. Amrita-Rus.

© Translate: Lidi Maryanovska

Cover image: Freydoon Rassouli

© Editorial design: Centre of Human Spiritual Development "Golden Race".

Published by CosmUnity

ISBN: 978-84-128563-0-9 (paperback)

ISBN: 978-84-128563-1-6 (EPUB)

Larisa Seklitova, Lyudmila Strelnikova

PEARLS OF THE HIGHER TRUTHS
Encounters with the Higher Cosmic Consciousness

This book is based on encounters with Higher Intelligence and highlights the questions of energy evolution for plants, minerals, and human body forms; along with the subject of our possibility for immortal existence. The reader of this book will find how the information received influences the development of the human shells [human physical and spiritual bodies], and how low Levels impact the perfection of souls in a negative way, along with damaging effect of ignorance, in addition to many other details.

Notation: (…) – Author's foot note.

[…] – Translator's foot note.

* – See glossary at the back of the book.

Part 1

CHAPTER 1

APPEAL TO HUMANS

Be sensible! Never become discouraged, malicious, lazy, as your soul must feed on the energy of the high spirit day and night. Nevertheless, most of you are too busy thinking about how to provide for your mortal body. You were created not solely for this purpose, and it is not for this purpose that We are nourish and cherish your Earth and you.

You, humanity, must realise your divine destiny and your supreme essence, as without it your life on Earth will be empty, bleak, and hopeless.

Wake up, humanity, and come to your senses and see the light!!! You are blind and you are proud of your blindness. How can you live the way you are living now? You have been given the best, but you are turning it into the worst; and you have been treated with kindness, which you are turning into evil. Your souls are plunged into the dark, hopeless, murk of ignorance, and none of you, with the rare exception, are pausing to think why you are alive and what you should do to be useful to God, Universe, Earth and to Humankind.

Get rid of your selfishness. Nothing humiliates a human as much as the small and detached world that he has created for himself, and now he is afraid to lose it. In order to preserve it longer, he applies all his efforts and thoughts, and dedicates all his energy and his time to this illusionary scrap of his existence. How can we open your eyes to all the beauty and fascination of the Cosmos [Universe] and the world that surrounds you?

You are so used to digging into your own dirt, not wishing to see and to know beyond what is occupying your mind.

Where can we find the energy and the words that might reach your hearts in consciousness and which might awake your souls from a deadly sleep, so you can be taken away from false aspirations and toward sublime ideals?

You have surrounded yourselves by illusionary goals and you have filled your lives with vanity and empty pastimes that do not serve your souls. It is extremely hard to reach for the soul and to guide it onto a true path. Even now, some souls are incapable of perceiving the sublime and the holy. Therefore, Sodom and Gomorrah are just pitiful flames compared to the fire that might embrace your Earth to burn all accumulated filth. It is in your hands to stop what lies in wait for you ahead.

Come to your senses and stop yourselves in your madness! We are calling on you to see Us, who came to save you! Let all your souls be pure and your thoughts full of light, and let you not follow the path of those unwise beings that dwelled on Earth before you. (Appeal of the Hierarchs of Earth).

(Appeal of the Hierarchs of Earth).

COSMIC (UNIVERSAL) LOVE

Question: Can a man of Earth understand what love in the Cosmos [Universe] is?

The Hierarch answers: The earthly man's understanding is primitive, often replacing the sublime with a baseness derived from the animal kingdom. Humans are made in such way that the earthly love granted them can only attract together the two halves that are presented as opposite genders in your world. This design is the same for all humans on Earth and for majority of non-earthly beings with physical bodies.

However, your program possesses a speck of cosmic love that manifests itself through love toward children and toward your nearest and dearest. If you have had only cosmic love, humanity would not have existed in physical form; hence, procreation; because cosmic love is an all-embracing love of all that is alive; and everything in the Cosmos is alive.

Your earthly origin would have disappeared due to excessive love toward all people; so, speaking in your language, everyone would have loved all people at the same time, which contradicts the scheme of physical evolution. Cosmic love can only exist on Higher planes, where it fulfils the function of unification.

There are worlds out there that only have cosmic love. All highly evolved entities belonging to the Hierarchical level possess it. There are also highly evolved genderless entities who produce children at predetermined times, independently from their desires. Every world is different. Many do not need physical love; therefore, they understand universal love, and it is not because they are genderless. These beings were created many millions of years before humans; therefore, they achieved high intellect and developed high spirituality.

If humankind were to fulfil our expectations and reach the same Level of perfection, then perhaps cosmic love might be understood by humankind, but not fully: it will be understood to the extent that is allowed by the program.

Question: If cosmic [universal] love is all-embracing, what does it represent in a broader sense of understanding?

Answer: Yes, the concept of cosmic [universal] love has been given to humankind in a form of all-embracing love. Any human being should be able to love all that coexists on the planet. But this concept exists only in the theory, as no individual can develop such an ability due to a lack of development.

An example of cosmic [universal] and all-embracing love toward all living things can be observed only in entities with remarkably high morals. It presents itself in the form of helping others and passing knowledge and everything else to those who are loved. This is a complete self-giving to others; this is creating and forgiveness at the same time, fighting for someone, and living in the name of someone.

Cosmic love is much stronger than earthly love. Its power has more might and its qualities are superior. Whilst earthly love connects only two people, universal love can unite a whole galactic community. Like the force of gravity, cosmic love can bind all members of a community into a strong relationship and to make them work as a single, unified, organism. Therefore, the growth and development of such society are much more advanced compared to one where there is an absence of universal love bonding. Societies without universal love have many more frictions and struggles over personal interests, which are slowing down progress regarding the development of civilizations. Only solidarity and unified goals, and cosmic [universal] love are allowing a jump forward into the future on the path of progress.

In societies where Cosmic love is present, it creates miracles and banishes disregard and deformity; there is no unhappiness or suffering, just as there is no selfishness or individuals fighting against the community as the things created are made by all and belong to all.

In the world, where everybody loves everyone, every individual reaches their maximum potential, as nobody supresses or creates obstacles, in fact the opposite is true: those of high rank help those of low rank to reach their highest level, because the goal for everyone is to help those next to them. Whilst common interests and goals can unify only for a short while, love creates a connection that lasts forever. The power of unification resides in love.

Because cosmic love spreads out toward everything around it and not only to what is similar to it, it strengthens the forces of creation. Love creates amazing worlds and paints them with pure and radiant colours that are both blissful and heavenly. However, these worlds are not just places of rest, work too must be done in them.

All beauty creates love, and all hideousness creates hatred; these are two separate qualities that belong to two opposite patterns of development. Love creates, and hate destroys. Love inspires and bestows everlasting light; hate suppresses and casts into the murk of impenetrable darkness.

Thanks to cosmic love, and its Divine part of creating new souls, these are created to be eternal. The great love of the Creator cannot destroy and erase them to dust forever. The matrix is everlasting. Only its qualitative expansion might be changed in the case of failed soul.

Based on cosmic love toward all living things, a whole Universe is built in a way that nothing in it dies, but transits from one developmental Level to another.

An example of Supreme universal love is Divine love. The Creator passionately loves everything that is created by Him and does not allow it to vanish and disappear without a trace. He lovingly cares about all and everything, including the most disgusting and vile things, giving them the chance to evolve, so even unworthy scum has a chance to rehabilitate.

The first step to cosmic love may be found in the phrase 'Love your enemy as yourself.' Whoever can learn to forgive enemies and to be compassionate and loving toward them, will understand the basics of cosmic love integrated in the foundations of the development of a whole Universe.

According to Supreme love, nothing vanishes even in the physical world: one type of matter [substance] transforms into another, one type of energy evolves into the next one. There is no destruction of substance, only its transformation. The process of reshaping the molecules and atoms of one substance into another with its effect on the influence of states and time, manifests itself as an endless evolution in the progression of a physical world. Let us consider a building. As time goes by, it is demolishing, leaving an unpleasant view. As the result, only dust and sand are left. But the dust and sand will add to the soil by becoming a substance for a new beginning, and this process is endless.

Love spreads the seeds of immortality and non-perishability in all that is created; and this is the most important characteristic of great cosmic love.

The utmost importance is to promote life, and death is a brief moment of transformation from one state into another, a state that each time becomes more perfect than the previous one. Death is perceived by humans as something horrible only because humans do not know the real order of things in the Universe; so that there is no death in Cosmos as such, just the transformation of one matter into another, and the cross-over into the next evolutionary level by Entities [Beings]. Similarly, there is no death for the soul in the spirit worlds, but only a transition; there is no destruction in the material world but reformation.

Based on cosmic love, the Creator takes care to preserve all living things alive eternally, but in evolution. As human societies progress, there will be no fear of transition, as there will be no incarnations and no necessity for reincarnation, (that can only happen after going through the appropriate evolutionary cycles which are the sixth and seventh civilizations on Earth [we are fifth]). Only further perfection [improvement] will allow humans to understand a true cosmic love that is creating, dignifying, and forgiving.

THE ILLUSION OF HUMAN IMMORTALITY

The golden dream of a human is to achieve the immortality which humanity has been seeking for thousands of years. Nevertheless, nobody has ever visualized precisely how to be immortal among all the mortals if one were to be suddenly blessed with such a gift.

The human does not think how tragic it is to live when everyone else around him such as friends, relatives and loved ones are dying, and he is the one who endures. He survives everybody who has known him, and then he must begin forming new ties and new acquaintances and try to be fit for the new times... Could this be fascinating?

One of the main factors binding an individual to a particular place, city, home, and work is family and friends, those he holds dear. Thus, as soon as these relatives and close members of society have departed from the state of living, and everyone else, foreign to him, have endured, the soul starts feeling unwanted and abandoned and the goal of existence wanes, so life becomes dead and empty.

Every human fits into a familiar circle of people. When a person is no longer its focus, he disappears from the spiritual realm of society and gets lost in the world.

A human never considers the psychological aspects of his existence, nor does he value them. Yet, they play a significant role in his life. Should immortality be needed if you are becoming unneeded? Should you be like an irrelevant shadow? It is as if you ended up playing the role of a homeless person who had fallen out from his circle of human affections because he did not appreciate them. He wanders among the living as a pitiful shadow. The feeling of loneliness and of not being needed destroys a human. A homeless person does not live long, and the reason for that is not so much because of a lifestyle, but because the psyche of a person starts working on suppressing life functions and leads to destruction.

In situations such as this, the reader may suggest that his loved ones be made immortal as well. However, there is always high price to pay for immortality, which can be afforded only by a few. If immortality is regarded simply as an extension of life, then psychological aspects will play no role, as a hundred or two hundred years of life are not considered immortality, but an extension of one's incarnation* (see glossary). Nonetheless, we are talking about eternity.

An immortal man will feel like spiritual outcast. He will witness the changes in time, generations, cities, and landscapes of the planet;

however, he will stay outside of them, as he is not connected to any of these psychologically. By becoming immortal due to some manipulations, he falls out from his personal program and loses the interconnection with the world possessed by everyone who lives by their own program.

The psyche of a man is usually attuned to a particular time, and in accordance with his program. For this reason, a human can sense the modern style in everything; for example, he can distinguish changes in music and see how some songs become old and others bring new energies with them. Being able to perceives time, he knows which clothes and fashion have become outdated and which ones are modern, and so on.

When one has endless life on the earth plane, the sense of the time intensifies more, and everything can only be glimpsed like on calendar pages.

Most things will be perceived differently by immortal men and mortal ones. But the main point is that the former will always feel estrangement from society due to them being built from different energies. And society will perceive such humans as somewhat alien, so it will not be easy for them on the spiritual plane [spiritually].

What if a group of people were to become immortal and attempted to build a happy life by helping others to become immortal: what kind of people would those be? Would they be the cleverest, most decent, or richest ones? All goods on Earth, in the first place, are at the disposal of those with lots of money; consequently, it is foreseeable that these types of people would attempt anything to become immortal.

That immortal sages could be heads of state is out of question since they would never be allowed to stand in power. As long as billionaires exist, all the best achievements will belong to them.

Let us imagine that a few decent people have managed to become immortal. Their decency would vanish once they realise their advantages and invincibility over others. They would change psychologically. They could not be killed, exterminated, or poisoned. They would glorify themselves because of their new state which is unusual for mortal individuals. Just like the beggar becomes too proud of wealth when he suddenly inherits it. The beggar is unable to manage his riches, and soon he wastes them. Thus, everyone should ask themselves whether they can manage their immortality.

Many times, I have seen the changes in a person when they become rich. When one is poor, they are quiet and humble, but when the money arrives, it is very surprising to see a metamorphosis from decency to indecency. They are completely new person! Even in the short term, a human can change qualitatively into their opposite. Hence, we can never be sure that once immortal, the human will stay the same as before: kind and decent.

As soon as the advantage of immortality over mortality is understood, one would try to concentrate power in their hands, and to become the lord of the world. It would be even easier to achieve this as a group of people. In striving to attain world power, they would eliminate all who disagreed, and leave everyone else as their mortal slaves. Good intentions would grow into a **worldwide evil**. So, it would not be a worldwide immortality, but worldwide slavery. People would be in servitude to those who were immortal. And never would immortals wish to share their blessings with others; this is an illusion. Modern man's low developmental level would disallow him to share it with others. The level of developmental progress, precisely, dictates the behaviour of a man.

If the scenario of immortality is to be granted for all living things on Earth, it would encounter its own problems. I am not talking about the resurrection of dead, as this is not allowed by reincarnation theory. How can resurrection take place if the soul is being born once again in a different body? Nowadays, because of the final appraisals of a soul's qualities, immediate reincarnations are taking place; so, it becomes possible for the soul to be born in a new body only a year after [death].

Let us further imagine that immortality is granted for all living things on the planet. The moral question then arises: should killers, rapists, and evil and brutal people be allowed to be immortal? And who will determine whether one individual deserves to be immortal, and another is not?

Humankind once again can be divided into mortals and immortals that will start a wicked war between themselves.

Moreover, no human being can appraise the person next to him correctly and to look into his soul. Only Celestial beings can do it.

People can deceive everyone, including themselves. They "pose" as righteous whilst harbouring wickedness inside them. The human is unable to see it; therefore, no tests can assist in revealing the righteous. Evil can easily camouflage itself pretending to be good. If indecent ones were to become immortal, should we not consider the future that would follow?

These are all psychological implications of immortal existence for some individuals, among others who are mortal.

If only man knew about the plans of Celestial beings, he would never have questioned the possibility of immortality for contemporary man. And let us continue this discussion further.

Look at immortality from a different angle.

To begin with, immortality has two types: in the subtle [spiritual] body or energy form, and in the physical body.

Talking of immortality, a human always takes his physical body for granted, as he simply cannot imagine surviving in a different form: the energy form.

A human can achieve immortality in his subtle body when he is perfecting his soul intensively. Some people successfully fulfil their individual programs from one incarnation to another, and then quickly proceed through hundreds of Levels of earth plane development. As they are successful, they are being transformed into an eternal existence on the Levels of the Hierarchy of God. These individuals have worked hard to perfect themselves so they can have an immortal existence. They are simply deserving of it.

Yet, this type of immortality occurs in the subtle matter [spiritual body], which is none other than energy. Every soul will eventually achieve this type of existence: some will achieve this earlier than others. Thus, **a human has the potential to be immortal, but he does not know it.**

Not understanding the principles of survival in the subtle world, a human strives for eternity in his material body, and in the same image [form] that he usually has at the present time.

Large sums of money are invested in some countries into research and development of the means to extend life; and there are some scientists who have achieved some results in supporting the active condition in cells that prevents aging.

A human rejuvenates himself in most cases by artificial means, such as plastic surgeries, which help the skin to look radiant. These are hopeless attempts to extend youthfulness.

The latest news is of a rejuvenation helped by numeric codes which is a human's attempt to be able to regenerate his body systems. To be exact, this is an experiment of Superior beings that aims to teach an individual to control the functions inside their physical bodies through new methods of mastering actions of the energy of numbers.

No doubt, the experiments are helpful, and research is necessary. However, when doing something innovative, a human takes the credit for new idea completely for himself. But what would he achieve without Superior beings? We should always remember that the Teachers of humankind or the Medical system – in this particular case – are experimenting through humans. They do have a goal in front of them to make the material shell of a human soul to be long-lasting and similar to those in highly organized [highly developed] Physical [Material] Systems in other Universes. Thus, the Medical System, throughout a variety of experiments by earth's scientists and researchers develops methods of cells regeneration in the biological body.

Earth's scientists in their research see one thing, and Supreme beings see something else, and to be precise, much more. They do not wish to make a modern man immortal since they understand that at the current time this is simply impossible; however, the work of earth's experimenters will be necessary for them in a very distant future.

We must remember that Jesus has resurrected the dead, and so has St. Nicholas, the Wonder [Miracle] worker. However, two thousand years later, we have still not entered eternity in the material body, because this is not in the Divine plans.

A modern human cannot become immortal due to many reasons. Let us itemize them from the Greater goals perspective. Everything is explained by the demands of soul progression.

1. Humans are being developed according to programs [schemes; blueprints] that set the length of life ahead of time. A human lives as long as is deemed necessary by the Higher entities, and according to his karma* and developmental level. No human being will live even a year longer than is written in his plan unless permission is granted by Superior beings.

2. The inferior developmental level of a human will not allow for his immortal existence. When a human, even an advanced one, lives long, deterioration sets in, and this can lead him to be decoded [eliminated from evolution].

3. The moral of a human is not ready for eternal existence. If, at this stage, someone unravelled body regeneration methods, a continuous misuse of this would begin. Thus, Higher [Celestial] beings are unable to let such types of individuals live forever.

4. If we try to defeat time and to rule over it, the power over it can never be used for eternal life or immortality, since time always links with the individual program; and in doing so, it connects with the plans of Higher beings; so, it is for them to decide whether to extend or to shorten the life of a particular individual. The isolated influences of some individual toward time cannot be regarded as his ability to influence its flow. All sporadic occurrences that happen are meant for the humans to extend their cognition, and for certain goals of the Higher beings to be fulfilled. Besides, time is not exactly what a human imagines it to be.

5. The mastering of numeric codes will not help everyone at the present time to regenerate their organism, as these are still specific individual experiments. The fifth* race, or civilization,

represents itself as a multileveled society. The presence of primitive, average, and advanced souls is evidenced by the different quality of composition of their physical bodies. And each Level (or to be exact, each group at this Level) requires its own numeric codes for healing. One numeric code will not fit all, as both primitive and advanced individuals have a different makeup. Nonetheless, in the distant future (at the end of the sixth race and into the seventh race) this [numeric codes] will be a highly prospective method of rejuvenation and revival. Representatives of the sixth* race [sixth civilization] will be close to each other in their developmental level; therefore, their compositions will be similar. Additionally, to use regeneration methods, one must possess great personal energy. People of the future will have this energy due to them having to fulfil programmes three times more complex, and all they will have to do is to learn to use it correctly.

6. And the main reason that makes immortality impossible for a modern human is a low Level of development of the physical matter itself that is not ready for eternal existence just yet. Its molecular and atomic linking have not reached a stable level that could hold them existing together forever. (Numeric codes used for regeneration work only for a biological matter [body].) The physical matter itself must reach a certain evolutionary Level in order to provide eternity for the material body of a human. Once this Level is reached, and so is the corresponding structure and potential, the whole of humankind will be transformed into a stage of immortal existence naturally.

Immortality, however, is impossible in isolation or in solitariness.

A crossover into eternity by a whole civilization is possible only on condition that a certain limit in the evolution of physical matter has been reached.

Thus, it is too early to speak about eternal existence. There is a long way to go to reach it.

The question arises: why is low level of development preventing the human ability to achieve immortality?

Immortality places a big obstruction on the perfection of modern man's soul. If said man were to be given an immortal body, then, at the current developmental Level of humanity (we are not talking "individual personally"), it would end up supporting the degradation of individual; and instead of leading him into eternal existence it would lead him into eternal damnation, as the soul which deteriorates, or downgrades can be decoded.

Once a person finds out he is immortal, his growth will stop completely. Only a knowledge of mortal existence and death in unfavourable situations compels a human to fight for his life every day, because any day could be the last day. Fear of death accelerates the progression of the soul.

At the present time a human is progressing out from 'under the whip;' and his mind is searching constantly how to fight hunger, to keep warm, where to learn healing himself and so on. If immortal, the human would not require food: he would know the methods of getting energy into his cells and he would know the methods of reviving himself and his strength. He would use his free time for further progression. However, only a man at the higher developmental level can acknowledge this. A low-level man, if immortal, is just going to lie on his couch and watch TV without a single thought in his head. He will not have any desire to learn or to better himself.

A contemporary individual does not understand the meaning of his existence. Life itself has no bearing on him, which means he is not obligated to carry responsibilities for anything or anyone; as, in his opinion, his life is just random, and the events in it have no secret meaning. Everything happens just by itself, according to the circumstances or personal desires; therefore, his life is empty and dull, and he feels no Higher meaning in it. Even if an individual sets some goals for himself, they are perverted, and he comes to the wrong conclusions based on them.

For example, an individual sets himself the goal of becoming a famous artist, or poet, or scientist; so, he maps out a plan to achieve this result. He studies, and he becomes successful, which helps his progress. As soon as the sought-after peak in his goal has been achieved, the human stops his development and lives with his achievement; and soon after the adverse process begins, which is deterioration. A stop in the development itself is degradation. This happens because the essence* of a goal is not understood correctly. I am sure that most people do not understand their goals correctly due to society's distortion of spiritual goals.

The essence of any goal or target is the perfection of a human being's inner soul. An individual can only achieve something if he moves in his progress a step forward. Yet, a human usually determines his goal as an accomplishment of great success in life, without a thought to his soul and that it earns certain qualities in the process and thus progresses too. And no, not a single individual thinks about it.

Instead, he thinks about something else: his glory, the material goods he will acquire as the result, and how he will be worshipped by others. And this is a gross perversion of the goal. Thus, he aims to achieve outstanding professionalism to acquire unlimited materials rewards and not to perfect his soul.

All the above is just a perversion of Higher goals and better beginnings: from the positive merits of the soul (development of professional qualities), the human changes toward negative accumulation (chasing money and expensive things); thus, negative energies are building up in his soul. And if the pursuit of goods outweighs the positive qualities of pursuing professionalism, the soul can get to a negative System.

The human cannot develop endlessly on one Level, as there is always a Level stopper. The reader can argue that if Pushkin [a famous Russian poet at the beginning of 19th century] not died, he could have written many more new masterpieces. Why was he taken so early?

Constant development in one direction, even if it serves art selflessly at the beginning of the path, eventually leads the human who lingers far too long on this path, to snobbery and arrogance. It may not be visible to others, but the soul accumulates negative energies, and no human can resist being praised by others. Being praised or flattered brings damage to the soul. Thus, some creative souls, in the absence of other reasons, are taken before they start accumulating negative energies.

Teachers from Above give a human a wonderful goal to become professional, to build up high positive qualities, but instead, he acquires negative ones. And the perversion is visible in the individual's attempt to swap positive for negative, and high for low.

This is just a simple example of how the human distorts personal goals and fails to collect the energies in his matrix that the Celestial Teachers need. The longer he stays at the peak of his glory, the more negative energies his soul accumulates. Why would Higher beings allow him to continue this outrage for another three to five hundred years? And does a human ever think about what he would do in an eternal existence? Even in his short mortal life, is unable to occupy himself with something useful.

The reminder: **Short lives are given to a human in order to provide an opportunity for him to make more corrections to his development in his program**. As an individual constantly wanders off from the righteous path, so he must be returned constantly through the system of reincarnations to the initial point in order to allow his soul to earn the necessary qualities.

If we are to extend life spans to thousands or millions of years, the soul will deviate from the right path much more than during a short life; so, making corrections to an underachievement will be much more difficult or, mostly often, impossible. To make the corrections in small quantities is much easier, and it is easier to achieve the sought-after qualities.

Most people do indeed reduce everything in their life to the material goods, with which they substitute their spiritual values. And this is a serious deviation from positive progression to negative progression toward the Devil.

Notwithstanding, God creates and raises His souls not for the Devil but for Himself. He will not allow His souls to transition to the negative

Hierarch (the Devil) in large numbers. God will simply decode* them and put their empty matrix back into the life cycle.

The goals of God in this matter are to receive highly spiritual individuals for His Hierarchy. Therefore, stoppers that do not allow the souls to side track to the Devil in large numbers are always present. Thus, the souls will not be allowed to live forever the way they want: forever in contentment and pleasure, and in the never-ending pursuit of money.

Money should never serve as the main goal in life of a positive individual. It is only necessary to support a physical existence and to serve the soul's perfection. When money turns into a personal goal, the soul is either ultimately decoded or forwarded to the Devil.

Yet, it is permissible to earn money for your own education or for the education of children, to help charities, schools, universities, public health, and suchlike; in this case, money takes on a positive goal. But one must be very careful with money, so it does not enslave the soul.

While pursuing money, a human does not notice when the fight for existence and development has ended and deterioration or sliding into negative System* has begun. He cannot see the fine line that separates positive and negative.

Only a Higher conscience understands which direction to evolve toward; what is acceptable and what is necessary to reject. Therefore, before the transition into eternal existence, a Higher conscience must be reached, or, in other words, one must build it oneself correctly.

A Higher conscience can see processes which lead souls in positive or negative directions assisting their progress or regress; It sees the truth.

A human, on the other hand, is unable to control his own development. He sets his sights constantly on one thing, such as to become a famous historian, professional musician, a master welder, or a well-known voyager; and he brings everything else to a standstill. He does not think about making any further changes to his profession, or about doing something creative in addition. He achieves one thing, and then he stops or calls it a day.

The one-way direction of learning is too lopsided [one-sided] for the soul. It does not provide for fully perfecting, even with the achievement of high professionalism in a specific field. The matrix* [of the soul] must be filled with various types of energies. When a human studies only a single subject for all his life, then only one cell [in the matrix] is getting filled, and this is not enough for full development.

Besides, the matrix development is limited to a specific world. Once it gets filled, the soul is unable to achieve anything new further on in the same direction in this world. Even lopsided development demands the transition into next plane of existence or into a different occupation.

Taking into consideration that the soul must be given a comprehensive, all-round development, so it can understand the world that surrounds it better, it is obvious that it must constantly change professions and lifestyles in order to proceed from one Level* into another Level in an ascending manner. The cell structure in the matrix needs constant growth in degrees of cognition, as the cell builds hierarchically.

However, no one can raise their Level voluntarily, as nobody knows the direction in which one must proceed; and the millennial experience of humankind proves such. Thus, an individual achieves high professionalism (even if it is at maximum level) and then stops. The matrix cells of a good engineer are not much different from the matrix cells of an academic that works in the same direction, as the difference in their knowledge at the earth plane is tiny and is not noticed from Above.

Does an academic know in which direction he should develop further and what he has accumulated already in his matrix? Usually, he rests on his laurels, and the development does not move any further.

And only Above, Celestial Teachers can determine what he needs at the next stage of his development in order to achieve full-fledged growth. Thus, all matrixes are being looked through, and the quality and quantity of each cell's content is examined, after which it is decided what qualities are missing, and what types of the situations are necessary to include in his next life plan, so he can develop them. Therefore, a former academic can become a simple peasant, so he can supress his arrogance and develop qualities such as patience and love toward his neighbour.

And how could Higher* beings grant an eternal existence even for a highly developed intellectual if he is stuck on absorbing just a single energy type, when a full spectrum of energies needs to be accumulated? Usually, many of those who have achieved professionalism, are transitioning from it to a heavy dogmatism, as the quality that they have developed has become highly potential and mighty and begins to block all other sprouts of new growth. Thus, they transition from progress to regress; and if a conservative professional, for example, is to be given an eternity he will begin a fight with new and progressive movements, using his extensive, old knowledge base. No dogmatic can salute the new, because the new always breaks old rules and shows that some former truths are no longer facts. Can a dogmatic admit that his knowledge is based on the wrong truth?

If we take an uncomplicated professor from the 16th century, revealing to him his past knowledge, he will see it as naïve, or old, or amiss; and it will become clear that his past study contained minimal true knowledge in; and this will happen constantly.

It should never be assumed that knowledge may be mastered to perfection. Humankind moves forward, and new and newer information gets uncovered for them. And it is only natural that the knowledge we provide will be changed for newer, more progressive understanding, one day. This is the normal way for development to proceed. Any given information is correct only during a specific time period.

As we saw earlier, the human plane* of existence, whether it is high Level or low, is unable to understand how it can progress further. Both of levels stop at one thing: viewing material goods as their top aspirations.

And it is important to point out that the human can pervert even a concept of Faith, which he converts into a dogma, and his development in Faith does not go any further. The Celestial Teachers say:

"Faith is an accomplishing of your actions according to Our requests."

What type of faith is shown by the actions of killing people in God's name, which contradicts God's summon "One shall not kill"? Hence, the human is being reminded:

"The evolution of the soul does not reside in a conflict of opposites, but in patience, consistency, ability to collaborate, and in cognition of contemporary God and His Commandments."

However, because all the above gets violated, humankind, at this stage of its evolution, cannot secure an uninterrupted development for itself; and, consequently, immortality. It does not have a proper comprehension of the general principles behind the developmental movement of the world it is both living and developing in as well. Therefore, Higher beings are unable to grant eternal existence to those who do not understand the goals of common development of the whole Universe. Everything evolves in synergy, and everything is orientated toward the Higher goal.

In addition, there is one more factor due to which the dream of immortality for humankind cannot come to fruition.

Each life created requires resources. It is like the union of man and woman that results in children, who the parents must support until their offspring learn to provide for themselves. This is also identical with humans and God, who spend their resources, those related to energy as opposed to money. These resources cannot be squandered on those who stopped in their development; thus, deteriorated. A human must replenish this depletion for his existence; and he should never forget it.

Due to many reasons, a human's life gets interrupted from Above deliberately, in order to be guided in the direction of comprehending the new truth.

As much as a human strives to become immortal, he will not be allowed to do this at the present stage of human soul evolution. Certainly, he may rejuvenate himself slightly and achieve youthfulness; however, it is not in his power to outlive his time, as he is lacking knowledge and ability. Nobody was ever successful in deceiving the Higher beings. Whenever the end of the program approaches, a human will die, even in prime health; and there are many reasons for his death besides physical aging. He might have successfully sidestepped aging and sickness, but he will get into an accident; he may have effectively rejuvenated himself, but only to die in his sleep.

The program of a human determines the number of years he must live, and a human is unable to overcome the program's power. The reader might say that there are some lamas or advanced individuals that have secluded themselves in caves, where they have rejuvenated and come back after. Nevertheless, those are isolated, experimental cases.

I want to underline this: to be immortal, one needs to be at an adequate developmental Level of consciousness and at a corresponding developmental Level of physical matter [body] possessing a special composition capable of withstanding the mighty potential of the soul.

The potential of physical matter [body] must increase at the same rate as the soul's potential.

The matrix is a self-developing and self-erecting construction; and the cells of a human's physical body are expected to be self-rejuvenating. The correlation between the potential of the soul and the potential of a physical body must always be present, so the soul's evolution or development can constantly influence the body's.

No immortality is expected for humans in the next two thousand years. Moreover, the length of life for future humankind is to be decreased to fifty years due to the fifth race falling behind in its development, and due to the need to increase the circulation of the souls, making their incarnation more frequent in order to eliminate delinquencies.

SHOULD A HUMAN PURPOSE BE SEARCHED FOR?

Many methodologies have emerged lately to reveal children's abilities. They are designed to ease the development pathways available for the child, so he does not have to wonder what to choose, searching for his place and preferences toward something in life, but can walk straight forward toward a life goal and achieve remarkable success. However, bringing out children's talents and promoting their growth is only one aspect; showing a human his mission is another thing entirely.

One of my acquaintances made me the following offer: "Let's reveal to children their mission, so we can discover a *wunderkind* [a very talented, child genius]." However, let us focus first on the nature of the goal of the development and how the soul's evolution occurs. Can the progression of an individual's soul be helped by revealing his mission to him?

In general, we could talk forever about development and its implications. Yet, when we observe people's misunderstanding of the Higher tasks, there is no choice but to return to this subject over and over again.

There is no need to discover geniuses. They will reveal themselves by their unique talents. But where do they come from?

Let us recall information presented in our other books which shows that abilities and talents are not a gift from Above but earned by the soul itself; these are the specks of "gold" energy, which a human has gathered in a secret storage place of his soul matrix by a persistent work. Thus, the mastery level is explained by the quantity of energy, of a corresponding quality, accumulated in the matrix's cells. When not many have been gathered in the soul, the abilities manifest themselves only faintly, and when a lot have been accumulated – the person shines with talents. Therefore, it is not so much a question of uncovering the abilities as of developing them and of growing personal assets of the matrix.

Masterminds do emerge from souls that had developed successfully in the past and had acquired steadfast qualities. Further development in the same direction will provide a high-quality expert.

The robustness of talent comes from a diligence of the soul. God simply provides every individual with an opportunity to develop abilities, mastery, and perfection in themselves, despite any difficulties and hardships. While observing the diligence of each soul, God builds, as a reward, the main program of life based entirely on creating. In this case, many great musicians, artists, poets, and architects are emerging.

Yet, they become great not so they can bathe in the rays of glory and live in luxury. They become great so they can serve as spiritual example for young souls, who have just begun their development, and to be the kind of example that youth can aspire to reach. Everyone must achieve the same degree of excellence as an outcome of their development…but after the next few reincarnations.

It is not possible to achieve this perfection during one lifetime. Therefore, every individual must prepare himself for great work, and one day (if he would like that), he can become great in the eyes of subordinates. Moreover, some souls who have accumulated a very high consciousness during their development are turning down their "great" place because they understand its true meaning, its burden.

To spot a child's inclinations, no special methods or calculations are needed, but only a closer look at him. Any inclinations, abilities, or talents are tied up to the aspirations of a child (or his parents).

At the same time, parents are known to force their ambitions onto their children, meaning that they are forcing something on children that their program does not include; thus, they hinder with the child's acknowledgment of his own inner inclinations. Without interfering with a child, and only by observing him, his predominant dispositions will be easy to discover.

A child's ambitions are coordinated with his program, wherein the program sets the developmental goal.

(Vile desires, such as temptations, can be enforced by a negative System; therefore, it is necessary to understand the types of ambitions and where they are coming from).

Early life inclinations in children do not always serve as the determiner of their destiny. After all, **every phase in life corresponds with its own ambitions** and with its own abilities. The program of the development is built in such a way to support progress, and for that purpose an individual needs to be interested in something. Obviously, a six-year-old's interests cannot be the same as those of a twenty- or forty-year-old.

Thus, the whole life of a human is divided into certain periods, and for each period it includes interests that are appropriate for that Level (degree) of an individual's development and the conditions of the place where the individual is located.

Prior to the age of seven, a child can use the abilities that he acquired in his past life, for example: he can make very good paintings, dance well for his age, because he had done these things in his past. Such a child can be considered a *wunderkind*, since his abilities appear in sharp contrast when compared to a backdrop of other incompetent young souls.

However, this does not mean that his past abilities are needed as a main direction in his development in his current life. For the current stage, it is not enough for him to be a painter, musician, or poet. He needs to be developed further; so, despite the child's passions and talents, he becomes an attorney or a company executive; and those abilities that revealed themselves at an early age are to stay [with him] as accompanying ones [hobbies]. They help him relax in stressful moments and they beautify his life with the inspiration of creating.

These past abilities serve as the foundations to build a person's real high taste, his delicate subtle feeling for the supreme arts; and they serve as a base for an ability to appraise professionally the artworks of others, which is impossible to do without the similar knowledge accumulated in the past.

Sometimes, the past abilities of a human are blocked because in the present life his assignment is to master standard business relationships or to work in a completely different area. He is focused on the new; therefore, his past abilities will reveal themselves only as the preferences of his taste.

Often, before the age of seven, a child is given the opportunity to develop himself in a new direction, such as playing some instrument, learning a foreign language, mastering different kinds of sports, studying mathematics, chess and so on. Thus, we need to teach child everything that is possible. This will be either a continuation of his already-present abilities or the development of new ones. Both are essential. Everything requires being brought to perfection.

But how do we distinguish past abilities from those that have to be developed? Is it possible to do so?

Past abilities reveal themselves; however, the soul treats them with indifference, and it does not desire to develop them further. The future abilities, on the contrary, will awaken the desire to create and to work in this given direction all day and night, and they will awaken the desire to strive toward the actions that will help to develop the new skill, or toward further perfection of skills that are present already. Thus, a human will only be able to reveal his own abilities and talents, but never to determine the destiny of another individual because no one will let him look into another person's program.

In truth, some clairvoyants can see some situations in a person's life; nevertheless, these are just a few fragments of his future life. These may be permitted to be revealed specially, so an individual can develop insight into certain situations.

Revealing a human's destiny is not granted to anybody, as this is a mystery of his development. There are only a few solitary cases that are given from Above and their purpose is to guide peoples' thinking toward the right direction. Even for us, the missionaries, human destinies have not been revealed; although, during contacts [channelling Higher consciousness], many have attempted persistently to receive information about their missions. At one time, while answering the question for a member of the group, Higher beings responded that life would be too easy for a human if he found out the main goal of his existence on Earth. By the way, not all those who were present in our working group and who were mentioned in the book "Higher Mind reveals its secrets", were missionaries, and not all of them had Cosmic names. I am purposely not revealing who is who.

Why is it not desirable to tell a human about his mission? Is there any harm in that?

The point here is the following: a human must not know about his mission; but, instead, he must feel it intuitively and he must strive to achieve it. The essence of soul perfection is in the search and in making choices between good and evil. If a human can learn to listen to a calling of his own soul (which he usually misinterprets for his body instincts instead), then he can develop an intuition and perfect his ability to feel his individual program; thus, he can reunite with the plans of Higher beings, which is exactly what they are striving to achieve.

If an individual knew his mission, the effort of his life's quest would disappear, and many educational moments with it. He should be heading straight for his goal. Not knowing allows the shortcomings and faults in a human to be revealed, as during the period of seeking his goal he is provided with choice-making between good and evil. And this is very important, because when he does not know his past and when the memory of his past experiences is blocked, the individual can perform either infamous or honourable deeds, depending on what choices he makes. This has a great importance on determining the qualities of his soul.

At the expense of the choices made, the human scores his points and builds his inner contentment. He constantly stresses himself by seeking out what is preferable to do in one or another situation, and what decision to make. His brain is analysing, his soul is working, and the outcome will be drawn after his death.

Neither ranks, medals, nor titles will serve as an outcome for his life, but rather the qualities that his soul has gained at the expense of own aspirations and choices made. More than anything, God values the growth of the soul. However, it is easy to end up in a negative System with ranks and titles, meaning that one will end up with Devil, as the ways chosen to reach those accolades corresponded with that system's methods.

And even if we assumed that an individual's mission was to be revealed to him: what good would it do? Would it help toward a qualitative fulfilment of his program? Definitely, in this case, the task would be eased. This can be compared with a difficult task solution by a pupil: in one case, he is informed about the final result, and in another, it is unknown to him. In the first case, his search scenario will be eased. However, before a human can find his mission, he must do a lot and he must learn a lot.

Just by itself, the presence of a mission in one's program does not mean anything, as there are always challenges and competitors present. And if the situation is not resolved in a favourable way for Higher beings, your place in the society will soon be occupied by a different person, who has managed to resolve the tasks given to him successfully.

Every person who fulfils important tasks for society has his double. Therefore, we can conclude that a single mission has few implementers or, to be exact, few applicants. So, if nine of them are unable to fulfil a mission, only the tenth will succeed. Announcing a person's mission, therefore, does not mean that it will be fulfilled. The prediction can only come true in cases where a fortune-teller sees the situation attached to the main point [event] of this person's program. Nevertheless, a fortune-teller still may not fully understand it.

For example, it is possible to predict that someone will become a president. This scenario is included in his program. Nonetheless, such a prediction does not mean the road toward becoming a president is wide open. To deliver on such a prediction, the person must work persistently and for long hours; and he must learn a lot, understand a lot, and pass a lot of tests. And only when he gets ahead of his competitors in all of this, only then can he occupy the post that was predicted. As we saw earlier, not everyone's mission gets accomplished.

Also, there is one feature that must be mentioned. To complete any mission, there are certain conditions that must be met. In order for a person to fulfil his mission, it is necessary to have a certain environment, as without it no manifestation of a human with the specified qualities will occur.

A person can be told about his mission; however, because society has its own variations of its developmental methods that may depend on other individuals' choices, individuals can choose the way where the situations are not apt for this person's actualization. This means that society can develop a situation in which the actions of that person will no longer be needed. Thus, different persons with different skills will be required.

For example, there could be a need for economists and not for politicians, for originators but not for demolishers. So, there are many factors that can interfere with the revealing of a human's mission.

The matter of importance belongs to a social environment, in which a person will end up as result of his personal choice or society's choice when the whole society decides to follow a certain path due to a set of circumstances that will lead a certain result.

As the result of choice, many situations change qualitatively, such as when an individual might end up in a negative environment instead of a positive one. In everyday life, it will look like an individual has ended up with the majority of people from a negative System around him who are constantly supressing and hindering him from manifesting his own self. In this case, it is not the ability to create, but the ability to protect and fight against this oppression that will be of utmost importance. So, for these situations, society has a variety of ways to demand an individual accumulate qualities that are different from the ones that would have been needed for his mission fulfilment while on a different path.

Moreover, many peoples' missions change during the course of their lives. Today, a person may do one thing, but tomorrow he might do another. Life itself constantly transforms and rearranges; thus, demanding a human to adapt to new conditions. The range of human missions is very broad. There is no point in sticking to only the great and significant ones. One person's mission is to become a janitor, and the other's is to become a cook, and a third's is to become a farmer. And who can say that one of them is unimportant? All of them are required for the people, and thereby for our society and each of us.

Furthermore, it is harmful to orientate a person on high missions as it promotes the formation of negative qualities such as arrogance, snobbery, pride and so on, in many.

A person must not get fixated on his designations and his missions. He should remain the free creator of his world and his soul. It is not the mission that is important for an individual, but the honest fulfilment of his duties and a maximum possible development in the direction of his interest.

A human does not define his goals correctly and is forgetful about his spiritual development. The goal is not just knowledge, but professionalism and maximum understanding of the subject one must work with. And one must work not for money, houses, cars, and other material wealth, but for the perfection of soul; and not just his own but everyone's. All material wealth will stay behind on Earth and return to dust; all that is accumulated in the soul will either ease one's fate in the future or weigh it down.

The mission of everyone is to be a Human in the best understanding of this word, because God created this [human] form specifically to fulfil certain Cosmic goals, and He expects to see a human show kindness and mercy, along with compassion and love toward others. Any mission on Earth is directed toward the developing of a perfect individual and perfect soul that will be worthy of transitioning into the Hierarchy of God.

CHAPTER 2

THE ENERGY THEORY OF THE EVOLUTION OF MINERALS AND PLANTS

The whole Earth evolves over the time. And this is an outcome of the development of its material shell and soul. The material shell transforms to fit the demands of the constantly changing spiritual components of the planet. And in consequence there comes an interdependence: the advancement of the planet's soul causes the advancement of its physical body.

As we know, every evolution is bound to work with energies. All that exists on Earth converts energies of one kind into energies of another kind during the process of its vital activity; and lower frequencies always transform into higher frequencies, promoting the perfection of its own soul; and supporting the evolution of the energies themselves.

The transformations of any state coincide with the give and take of energy; thus, in some cases energy is spent and in others it is replenished by carrying out certain work. However, these are just generalizations. But how does the evolution of the atmosphere, the bio-field and the waters of a planet really take place?

Moving along from the fact that everything living evolves, inevitable changes will affect the sea and the air, since they are closely connected with all that is alive.

Being transformed according to the new demands of time, plants, animals, and humans, in the process of their life cycles, bring changed organics and microelements into the soil and breathe out changed gas compounds into the air. Additionally, they effect changes on the surrounding matter after their death, when they fall to the ground and disintegrate into new energetic compounds.

The atmosphere, moreover, has a certain subtle composition that allows gas elements to place themselves in a certain order from the surface of a planet toward its outer layer according to their density.

It would not be possible for the planet to hold the atmosphere in place, and for the atmosphere to be a permanent state if the atmosphere had no outer layer [shell] and a special, subtle composition. The force of gravity, by itself, is not enough since every wind and hurricane from the space would constantly blow it out of place and distort its composition.

The atmosphere has an order. The degree of its rarefaction and density is conditioned by the presence of subtle constructions that hold together certain compounds and concentrations and the required parameters of the outer shell of the planet. Similarly, human shells have a specific build and retain only the accumulations that match them. They also make provisions for a human's individuality.

In the same way, water (rivers, seas, and oceans) has its own subtle, structural build that allows the water masses to stay in their preassigned volume and places. The location of seas, oceans, and rivers on the planet is not random, but conditioned by the physical functions of Earth, additionally they are connected with the processes of distribution and accumulation of energy by the planet.

The atmosphere and the seas are not a source of chaotic movement of its constituent components. They have the specific mechanisms which allow them to participate in some processes and not to participate in other processes; thus, gathering a certain type of elements and not others into their structure. The physical processes are governed by the subtle mechanisms; and water, like atmosphere, has its own subtle skeleton that does not stay permanent, but is subjected to corrections over time.

On our planet, everything is so interconnected that a correction made in one place stretches out to everything else like a chain reaction; thus, nothing else stays at the same Level and in the same state. Therefore, even when global changes are taking place on only one layer of the planet, they gradually spread out to all other layers.

The changes in the seas, soil, and in the atmosphere can be seen even by the naked eye, as well as confirmed by laboratory research and by chemical and physical analyses.

Yet, how, for example, does the evolution of minerals take place, if, for humans, at the first sight, a rock remains a rock, unchanged in its structure and chemical makeup? Only its size can show changes. What concludes the development of the rock? Where is the evolution of minerals heading?

To answer these questions, we need to take a closer look at the rock.

If we take any mineral, then it is possible to observe, within even small segments of time, how some of them grow and change the form of their crystal structures. Quartz and rhinestone crystals grow, and over time, the chemical compound and structure of other minerals change; and this is either a process of development or a process of retrogression (regression; destruction). Either one means the evolutionary process in its two opposite states. The direction of energies upward is catabolism [assimilation], and their transformation downward is anabolism [dissimilation].

Evolution is a process of movement toward a higher energy Level, and involution is the crossing over onto lower Level. The transformation of energy toward either side is endless.

In the Universe, as on the Earth, nothing stays the same, and the fact that "everything flows and changes" is true for as many years as our world exists; thus, our planet today is very different from the way it was millions and billions of years ago. Lifeless and primitive at once, it evolved to such a degree that it became a highly developed and complexly organised planet.

How did evolution take place before, and how is it occurring now? What was its starting point?

Perhaps, we should start from the last question in order to see the integrity of the process, even if it just for a short period of time, as all that a human can see is always a part of something that has already been functioning for a while. Every beginning is approximate, but it serves as a convenient starting point. Therefore, an initial point for our evolution is not so much primordial, but hypothetical, so our knowledge is always just a fraction in the vast ocean of information.

Let us address the last question, though. The primary cause for Earth plane evolution was the starting of the program from Above; thus, the turning on of some kind of "start" button. The origin of Earth's evolution was, as astrophysics has affirmed, an explosion that turned a certain process into action.

In order for an explosion to happen, the volume in question receives a "starting" energy from Higher Entities*, who specialise in bringing the plan entrusted to them to life.

Inside this volume exists a predetermined number of primary elements, which are created and developed by Higher beings for the purpose of creating a certain kind of a physical matter. The explosion is needed to start the program, which then compels elements to bond and interact in such order that the world can start to be built.

The energy of an explosion is used to create the primary bonds. Further on, an extended process of building the chain of all kinds of space, galaxies, worlds, and after that –planets, begins. Then, the planetary systems, including the Solar system, are formed. And, according to the Higher beings' design, the Earth's material shell is formed at the required stage of Solar system development.

Without a doubt, humans can see a discrepancy in our information, as we said initially that Earth and its soul are created by God, and now we are talking about an explosion that served as the starting point in the evolution of the Universe and the world on Earth.

Needless to say, the matrix of the Earth and the matrix of the human soul were created by God and his Helpers. Nevertheless, for a human, the starting point for his development is his birth time, which is contingent, because preparation for his birth started long before his conception. Higher beings have orchestrated this preparation as well.

Similarly for the Earth, we assume the explosion as the starting point, which has formed the material Universe and the elements around it in the shape of the planets and planetary system from given physical matter. Earth appeared at a certain time during the Universe's development, and according to the program.

Everything was calculated, planned, and divided into developmental stages ahead of time, and every developmental stage is built according to the program and specific conditions, and all of it was planned from Above. This concludes the fact that every evolution is not random but is controlled and purposeful. A higher developmental level always governs the evolution of a lower plane.

Thus, each step in each world of minerals, plants, and animals and so on was planned beforehand, and did not appear spontaneously or at the will of "wise nature".

The evolution of minerals, as well as of plants, was scheduled way before it occurred. Nonetheless, deviations from plans did happen, but later everything was corrected through catastrophes, floods, the action of elements and so on. Worlds were being built and rebuilt.

The formation of different kinds of rocks (granite, basalt, marble, etc.) was developed specially, as well as the forms of plants (rose, lilac, cactus, pine, etc.) Special instructions, in which action mechanisms were focussed on special processes and toward the transformation of a specific spectrum of energies, were created for each kind of material form.

In addition, all forms underwent changes over time according to the demands of a changing environment and goals were set for them. The genetic code, implanted in the seed of a tree (which is its individual program), is to unfold the seed's structure over time, step by step, in the same way as in minerals. As time goes by, the processes in them change.

Individual programs govern the processes of minerals and plants. Some forms, after being created by Higher Creators by many complex processes, were set aside for Earth production, meaning that their individual programs were included in the Earth's main program. So, the planet started to create their material shells inside of it, but according to the goal that had been prearranged for her. This is implanted in the mechanism, where one organism gives birth to another; so, one physical form gives birth to another. It works the same in humans: one person gives birth to another once suitable conditions exist.

Certain types of minerals were created by the planet in particular conditions of temperature, moisture and pressure, and other types relate to different parameters. The amount of primarily preassigned elements, the parameters of environment, and their program were the regulators of the number of minerals.

Chemical elements have joined according to certain laws in their individual programs, creating atoms and molecules of specifically planned substances, which, in turn, have created minerals at the required environmental conditions and pressure. Then, amorphous and crystal structures were formed.

In this way, Earth has created the forms, in which, at a certain time, the matrixes of the souls that controlled their individual programs were implemented. These were the initial matrixes, with the basic sets of energies, which started to form an individuality of minerals and influenced the specifics of the processes in them.

Subsequently, intelligent and independent energy emerged in the minerals; and similarly, the processes that formed the composite of the future souls of rocks.

The development of minerals extends for millions of years. They are exerted to the influence of colossal pressures, temperatures, magnetic and electrical fields, and by many other factors that convert the primary energy inside them into an energy of higher quality. The minerals work for the planet. By performing some of the planet's functions, they have provided the planet with energy, and, at the same time, they have developed their own matrix. Each matrix shell then becomes gradually filled up with different energies through its own work processes. This is how the perfection of soul that came from the Earth plane began. This is how an evolution of Earth-type souls has begun. (We can consider the starting point for the evolution of such a soul, as either the insertion of soul into minerals, or the moment of matrix creation by Higher entities).

The minerals, in their processes, are always linked with the soul of the planet, as they provide normal existence for it by maintaining the planet's material form. The energy accumulation takes place in the matrixes of rocks and in the matrix of planet, so that the energy potential* is increasing in both of them.

Time can be regarded as one of the factors of energies' transformation, as without it no transformation could ever take place.

Under the pressure of many factors, which influence minerals on the outside, there is also the change in energy quality that occurs on the inside, and the initial [primary] energy being evolved. The minerals have an incarnation of the "soul" or an elaboration of energies in the different shells during a course of time, which implies their participation in various processes. In minerals, energy transformations take a very long time, and one process may last millions of years.

Energies of the soul are subtle energies, and not material nor physical. This subtle energy is produced in minerals during the process of their vital functions. In order to perform an evolutional, qualitative leap, it must achieve a specific magnitude, which produces the highest energy potential for their plane, or Level of existence, which then allows the energy to cross over to the next Level and into a different form of existence. It could be directed to the world of microorganisms or insects, or into certain types of plant species.

Minerals are not all equal in their developmental level. Obviously, those that have achieved a greater energy magnitude could be considered more developed. For example, one mineral over the course of two million years achieved three provisional units in its energy level, and another one, over the same time, had achieved forty provisional units. Naturally, the second one turned to be a more progressive, "smart" one; and as the result, the evolutionary process of these souls might accelerate or not in the future; however, the qualitative part of the energy of the soul will be improving during the same period of time.

The evolutionary leaps-transitions from one Level to another do not necessary occur at the same time for everyone. Above all, the transitions happen individually once the energies have become ready. Nevertheless, collective transitions also take place. During a specific period, an advancement of energies happens in the cycle, during a specific interval of time.

In the cosmos [macrocosm], there are functioning cycles that belong to the collective plan, and all worlds fall into line with them. The cycles play a dominant role in all that develops, and a common mass of progressive forms is adjusted to them during their development.

A whole chain of hierarchical Levels transitions during the time of collective leaps in the same way as school classes at the end of the year transition from first grade into second, and second into third, and so on; nevertheless, some may repeat a year in the same class.

On the Earth and in the cosmos, everything is much more complex, and, maybe, much tougher. During these leaps, all souls who are late in achieving a certain level of perfection are decoded [their individuality is wiped out and only a clean matrix is left]. They are not even being punished for an underachievement, but simply are being destroyed as failures; thus, it is very important to meet the developmental deadline on time.

At the same time, there are individual forms that outperform their counterparts in development. These are single replications of the most progressive forms that can transition to higher Levels using their own abilities, and their transitions are accomplished outside of cycles.

Going back to minerals. In order for the leap to happen, their evolution should have started a million years back and have prepared the matrixes existing in them for the needed requirements.

An individualised development allows for the single minerals to outrace other minerals in their development. But at what expense can it be possible? Certainly, the programs are of paramount importance in this matter; however, no individual programs are designed for this purpose. So, the question remains: how can one mineral outperform another during development?

Minerals, just like people, react differently to environmental conditions, such as the same temperature; therefore, the processing of physical energies and manufacture of subtle energies inside of them will be different, and the quality of energy received by the matrix will be individualised.

A specific trait of minerals' development is an absence of degradation. Nonetheless, they possess a mechanism to divide energies into positive and negative ones. Minerals can produce energy with positive and negative signs. The sign of the produced energy, or the process which will produce energy with a necessary sign, is imprinted in the program [for minerals] from Above, and the sign depends on the inner composition of the mineral.

However, starting at a certain developmental Level, a mineral can choose the direction of its progress, so it can develop energies of different qualities in itself. This allows minerals to develop their own individuality. I must underline again that the choice is only given once a certain Level has been achieved.

In the world of minerals as well as Levels there are divisions into sublevels, so it has a hierarchy. Thus, in the world of minerals, there are both young souls with a minimal accumulation of energies in the matrix and old souls with an extensive selection of energies.

Minerals participate in the different processes of the planet, and some of them accumulate more negative energies, while others collect more positive ones. Consequently, some rocks have a negative influence on people and animals (those with minus sign), and others, on a contrary, have positive influence (those with plus sign). The more the mineral resembles in its quality composition a human's quality composition, the more and better it will suit him.

Besides, minerals absorb human energy very well because they do not possess this kind of energy themselves, or to be exact, they do not develop it. Therefore, a person that has high power potential and thus high energy accumulations can hand over part of it to the stone, along with a certain affirmation for good or evil. It is in this way that a talisman is derived.

Minerals are connected with the planets of Solar system by their material energies. There are twelve types of these minerals. These are twelve types of physical energies, with which the minerals work [interact], depending on the minerals' type.

The processes that allow an energy exchange with the planet and with the physical types of energies of a living world are implemented in the rocks, including the ability to include the subsequent processes into a reaction, at the expense of which the transformation into the subtle energies begins.

The material types of transformed energies in the minerals correspond with those of plants, animals, and humans, who are also connected with the same planets, and who are also working on their physical range energies.

Thereby, the system of twelve connected planet divides our Earth into twelve zones, where each of them works on a predetermined frequencies range. Each connection in any zone produces the frequency that corresponds with its type, wherein all Levels of the planet are connected with each other by zodiac. Therefore, the minerals in zone "two" will produce the energy frequencies that will be necessary for the plants in their zone, and the minerals from zone "eight" will produce the energies that are necessary for their zone. And, at the same time, both can be connected with the planets in the Solar system working on the frequencies of zone "eight", and this interplay expands further into the worlds of animals and humans.

Thus, this is a complex interaction, where energies evolve not only through different worlds in the chain from the mineral to the human, but also through diverse ranges. In other worlds, the evolution of energies does not just go from top-bottom, but left-to-right.

The direction of "left-to-right" for our Earth is defined by twelve main ranges of frequencies, which correspond with the twelve Zodiac signs in astrology. Before understanding how the energies correspond with signs, we must understand the transformation of energies from top to bottom, from simple to complex, from the world of minerals to the world of humans.

Every world has its own transitional borderlines between one energy Level and the next one. The more advanced the world's Level is, the larger number of energies the members of this world should accumulate in order to transition a step higher. And every world has its own processes that support the emergence of the necessary energies inside the specified form.

During the process of evolution, the number of energies that participate in said process increases and, at the same time, the number of energies produced by a specific form that resides in this world is increasing too. For example, the number of energies in the processes involved in the evolution of minerals is less that in the processes involved in the evolution of animals, and animal evolution involves less than human evolution. Consequently, the spectrum of new energies produced by minerals is less than those in animals, and animals have less than humans.

Our investigations of the energy shells of minerals, fish, and animals have shown a steady development of energies, increasing their qualitative and quantitative potential, and raising the number of energy types involved in the evolutionary process (from the book "Revelations of Cosmos").

The subtle shells of minerals have ethereal shells (etheric body) and atmanic* shells (atman; spiritual body), while plants (flowers, bushes) have the additional energies of emotions and desires; and they develop sensual energy, energies of action, reason and effect, and energies of protection and counteraction as well.

In grass, as in minerals, the reason-effect shell is absent, because the processes involved in a further transformation of energies of this plane are not yet engaged in their work. However, spiritual energy is detectable in grass, flowers, and trees. The "spiritual" energies, of course, are a conditional name, since they get accumulated not through some special spiritual activity, but through the specific processes inherent to specific forms.

Spiritual energies are energies of a maximum high quality for any given Level or Sublevel of existence.

Some plants produce them, and some do not, meaning that they need a long period of time in evolution in order to start producing spiritual energies.

If we speak about the presence of thought processes in minerals or trees, a human immediately will associate this with his own thinking. Yet, various forms have processes which are a match for human thinking activity as a mechanism to process certain types of energies. But these mechanisms are completely different; therefore, humans can never understand the thought processes of minerals and trees, and they also cannot understand how the thought process takes place in a human. After all, at this stage of his evolution, humans cannot understand the thought processes of Entities, who do not have physical brains, in the subtle worlds of God's Hierarchy*; yet their thinking is much more advanced in magnitude than human thinking. Thus, the question is only about which processes are to be considered thought processes.

When observing the plant kingdom, which is also hierarchical, we can see that the energies humans consider belonging on a mental plane, are absent at the lower Sublevels of plants (grass, flowers, and bushes); yet, they are present at higher Sublevels, such as trees. The energies of the mental plane are accumulated in tiny specks by the archetypes of lower planes.

The practice has shown that new types of energies, such as mental, and cause and effect, are appearing in some specimens of the flora. Where are they coming from? Had they already been implemented ready-made from Above?

Not at all, those types of energies are not installed into the shells, but the mechanism of processing material energies into subtle energies is. The higher the Level where the energy that needs to be produced is, the more complex the process of transforming it. Thus, the program of a form becomes more complex, and likewise the complexity of the mechanisms involved in the process.

For example, in order for primitive thought processes to start working in a tree, the tree is given a special program, and a device is added to its subtle shell which can react to certain situations in the life of the tree such as specific indicators of atmosphere and the surrounding environment.

These situations are absent in plants, contrary to a human; however, they do react to the slightest changes in the environment. Their program includes indicators of normalcy, which, when present in the environment, allow the plants to feel comfortable. When these indicators deviate from the norm, established in the program, the defensive forces of organism take a stand. In order to survive, the plant starts resisting negative influences and realigning chemical reactions and physical connections, and so on. Thus, an adjustment to new indicators takes place.

The plant conducts difficult work, which is unseen by a human. In particular, in higher [advanced] plants, mental energies step into their work. No doubt, a tree cannot think like a human does; yet it can operate mentally in its own way, when it is reaches a particular Level of its development.

In order to implement higher processes into the form, form must develop to a certain stage and to accumulate necessary content in its matrix. Without this condition, the form will be unable to transition to advanced and more complex processes. In order for thought processes to start working, the plant must rise to a certain Level, or, to a certain energy potential in its matrix. This energy potential then will set mental energies in motion. Then, the plant will have enough strength and might for the governing processes that coincide with mental activity.

In order to awake the ability to think (to work with the energies of a certain type), or any other high [more advanced] process, the subtle mechanism that helps the form evolve in advanced processes according to its program, is added into this form's construction.

New constructions are only added into the subtle shell in a case when the form has gained the necessary accumulations in its matrix, and its energy potential has achieved the might that can set this new mechanism in motion. This is how a form's transition to a new type of activity takes place.

To understand this principle better, let's refer to an example with an animal. The design of an animal's physical brain is constructed to perform certain primitive processes. In order to increase the thought processes of an animal, its soul is transitioned into a human form, which has expanded the work principle of the brain apparatus. The transition from one form to another happens once a lower form has achieved a certain stage in their development.

Even though the thinking apparatuses of humans and animals are alike; their abilities are different, due to the more complex build of the human apparatus. Forms for these corresponding levels of development are constructed by Higher [Celestial] designers. Each form is orientated toward work with a certain energy range. This is very important, as it will condition the form's structure.

Above is an example of the soul transitioning toward working with different processes during the process of perfection. But let us return to plants. There are evolutionary steps in the world of plants; therefore, a soul evolves through being grass, then through stages of being a flower, bush, and a tree; and then it transitions to a group of reptiles, insects, fish; then birds, small animals; and then to big animals; and, finally, to humans. Accordingly, a soul can be reborn into the same species several times, as each type has its own Sublevels of ascension. Thus, according to the energy levels, there are low-level [primitive] grass and high-level [advanced or superior] grass, and low-level trees and high-level trees, and so on.

In this way, the subtle energies produced by minerals continue their development at the next steps of the plant and animal worlds.

Nonetheless, not all matrixes from the world of minerals will transition into the world of plants. Some minerals are strong, and some are weak. As was described above, some minerals are so successful in the process of energy accumulation, that their might is too strong to be held in a plant's physique. Thus, the matrixes of ex-minerals are sent to different worlds or to the Earth plane in forms that correspond to their Levels, where their power can be sustained inside new material forms.

But in any case, a further progression of the soul takes place. The possibility that not all souls will undergo a necessary transition from the subordinate plane to the superior plane, applies to different Levels. Individual souls there can be transitioned into completely different worlds either because they need to accumulate certain qualities, or because of the demands of higher goals. Thus, every rule has an exception; however, these exceptions obey Higher purposes.

The souls that are being transitioned must continue their progress. Thus, abilities, qualities and life experience are increasing, and gradual accumulations of the energies of corresponding plane by the matrix takes place.

The same is true in the plant world. Some of their souls could be transitioned to the different worlds, where they will accumulate a non-Earth range of energies. However, the plants that compose the Earth's plant Level, work with the material [physical] type of energies. Based on their transformation, plants produce subtle energies according to their range and Level. Because of special mechanisms implemented in them, low energies transform into high energies, and this is a gradual evolution of the souls and energies themselves.

How do the processes of transformation occur?

From what was said earlier, once the soul's matrix has achieved a certain degree of its potential, the soul transfers from one form into another, which has a more complex structure that orientates the soul to work with the energies of a higher order. Nevertheless, every development, stage, and step are fulfilled according to the program. The physical form's program joins the matrix's program, and both start working mutually, filling cells with the required energy types.

The gene code of a plant expresses the program of its material [physical] shell. However, the matrix connects only with the seed whose gene code gives a signal to turn on the material program. This means that when the seed is in normal conditions, the development program turns on in it.

The gene code, or the material shell's program, steps in to work; and at this time there occurs a reunification of the soul's matrix and material body. In order for the material plane's program to take place, the presence of certain external conditions such as a calculated atmospheric pressure, temperature, and so on, must take place. The sum combination of necessary factors creates the force which sets the program in motion, and the seed starts to grow. The deviation of even one preassigned factor from the normative indicators, imprinted in the program, results in a non-occurrence of the physical body's program launch, and, eventually, the seed dies.

If a seed's life cycle is started, it works toward its own life support, and as a result, the material energies, participating in the process, transform into a new type of subtle energies. Plants, as we noted above, have emotions and feelings. Even grass can perceive an aggression, malice, or kindness in a human, through contact with him, and will react accordingly.

Plants experience horror and fear when an individual approaches them with bad intensions. Thus, if they are experiencing such feelings, then they are equipped with the processes and mechanisms to transform material energies into the subtle energies of the astral plane [emotions' plane]. Also, they have methods of transformation [of energies] on their subtle shell's plane, which are not known to humans at this time. All above there are various mechanisms of engaging astral plane energies in the work and their transformation.

If plants experience fear, they can counteract toward the source of fear with their own methods; for example, some plants emit a foul smell, others become covered with droplets of moisture, and yet others shed their leaves temporarily. When a plant either counteracts or perceives something favourably, it accumulates the subtle energies of cause and effect; thus, the energy of a certain range is produced.

The trees are the mighty [powerful] representatives of the plant kingdom; therefore, the processes and situations that allow rudiments of thought processes to emerge are included in their development program. The processes are implemented in physical matter and in a body's gene code; and the situations are planned inside the program of a soul. In trees, for the first time, mental energies start to appear and work; however, in grass and bushes they are still absent.

In a tree, moreover, the energies of the casual plane [physical actions] are included in work more. All of this is conditioned by the structure of the physical shell and the subtle bodies. No evolution of physical plane energies can occur without their special construction. As we can see, only the special structures and mechanisms, which are able to transform low frequency energies into high frequency ones, can participate in the evolution. And the most important fact is that the Higher beings' thought [Higher Thought] participates in the evolution.

Thus, every form in the chain of evolution is designed to consume, to transform, and to produce certain types of energies. Said forms always consume low [inferior] energy and produce high [superior] energy (but only within their own range). Thereby, energy of a certain quality and quantity is being produced. The quantity is correlated with the needs of a planet and the goals of its development and existence.

Besides, there is a steady accumulation of quality energy by the soul that demands gradual transformation through the specific qualitative accumulations, for which one or another form is calculated for. In order to produce the required amount of energy by one form, the methods of repetition, or reincarnation*, must be used. They make possible for an increase in quality of accumulated energy to be attained by the soul, and they promote an intensive circulation of energies.

Souls, whilst evolving themselves, are helping the evolution of the physical matter with which they interact, as everything in the world is interconnected and interdependent. Souls and their constructive build [structure] are the most important mechanisms of the transformation and evolution of the worlds and energies in our Universe. Without them, no evolution could take place.

THE EVOLUTION OF HUMAN'S BIO-MATTER (BIOLOGICAL FORM)

The evolution is comprehended through comparison; therefore, one may consider the example of pharaoh, who lived before our era, and a modern human. Even though we perceive a human organism as unchanged during the last five thousand years, it has endured great changes, and especially during recent times.

The Hierarch, referring to the third and fourth civilizations, talks about reconstructing the human form.

"They turned away from the main goal, given by Us. As a result, and, in Our understanding, a whole Earth civilization has deteriorated. Thus, for Earth, the new and improved forth civilization, which corresponded with Our demands, at least for some time, was created. Nevertheless, as all the previous ones, it had its own faults in understanding Our goals, theories, and interpretation of Our information. (Ninety percent of the information received had distortions)*. We smoothly reconstructed them [humans], considering the newest demands of the System [Cosmic systems; Cosmos]. And this civilization [the fourth] has transitioned partially into your fifth civilization.

However, once again, We are acknowledging our mistake, and We carry on, once again, smoothing the correction, without destroying a whole civilization, even though some Systems are vouching for the destruction of Earth.

Despite this, We are hoping that new forms will be so progressive that they will be able to transition to the seventh and eight civilizations simultaneously.

Their composites* are compounded together, which did not happen in previous civilizations. This human model will assist humans to move forward significantly in evolution. These people will be ingenious in all dimensions: mental, physical, and spiritual. These people will not only hear their Determinant [Spiritual guide]* but will collaborate with him as well.

They must rise to heights that no one of five civilizations has ever achieved before."

Yet, even if the High goals of our Creators were not to be considered, it is reasonable to suggest that when the world starts changing, the physical body will not remain unchanged.

Its outer structure has stayed the same, but the quality content of bio-matter has changed. Every cell of the organism has changed, and its energy transformed; along with all the chemical processes and reactions going on the inside that have changed too. After all, the human ate different food and drank different water before (the chemical composition and energy of these have changed over time as well); therefore, previously the endocrine glands disintegrated substances that were totally different to the ones they do now.

In addition, the energy that has been sent out to the human by his Detriment, has changed. Two thousand years ago humans received energy that differed from the energy a modern human receives now. The energy potential sent was increasing steadily. When a human receives new energy, then all his body's processes start working on this new energy.

The energy enters the cell which includes it in its processes. Inside the cell, new chemical and biological reactions start taking place, but now on new "fuel", and at new energy base. The chemical reactions start building on new energy, promoting a "recharge" of molecules, and then atoms, which also are transitioning to a new energy Level. New energy expands deep inside the substance of matter and deep inside the particles from which this matter is being built. An increased growth of potential of the matter takes place, and this is what promotes its evolution. At the current time, even the valence of chemical elements changes. And this relates to the Earth's transitioning to a much higher energy Level, to new stage of development; thus, evolution involves [influences] everything.

The changing worlds of plants and animals, humans' large scale industrial and agricultural enterprise has changed the chemical composition of water and soil. By damping waste and washing chemical substances into the fields, humans compelled them to change. The soil changed and water forced plants to mutate, which influenced further changes in animals and humans.

A case in point is that concentrations of all kinds of chemical agents in the soil and in wells have increased so much toward the end of the twentieth century, that everything around has become poisonous.

If a human from a thousand years ago or even from three hundred years ago were to be transported to our conditions, he would get poisoned immediately and die in a few days. The reason for his sudden death is that his bio-structure is absolutely unprepared to deal with modern chemical and organic compounds, because even though he looks the same as a modern human on the outside, his inner energy content and all of his processes are completely different.

His endocrine glands are working at a different rhythm and are designed to work with a completely different chemical composition of food; and in the same way, his cells have a different subtle structure; and, therefore, produce different energy.

Celestial beings improve constantly upon the modification of human structure. Just as a TV cannot stay unchanged for dozens of years and models are improved each year; likewise human construction is modernized constantly and evolves from one civilization to the next and from one nation to another. What changes especially are humans' subtle structures and cells of their bio-structure.

Each cell is a whole autonomous area, which consumes one type of energy and then transforms it into another type. The cell is feeding, breathing, living and procreates; it has its own subtle shells, its own individual program and personality, and its own destiny.

The human, as a whole, is composed of cells, but can we say that heart and kidney cells are identical? They both have individual inner structures, different programs and functions, and different goals. In effect, heart cells cannot work in the same way as kidneys cells, and vice versa; however, they possess interchangeability; thus, when one organ becomes disabled, the other organs pick up its load partially.

Nevertheless, the functions of the cells of various organs in one organism remain as individual cells.

Yet, why is the human model changing over time? What causes it to improve asides from Higher beings changing humankind's goals and its deviations from the program?

Firstly, it is connected with the soul increasing its energy potential. Each civilization has had the human model that was calculated according to the civilization's energy Level and the maximum magnitude of energy potential which the model had to accumulate by the end of its existence. Therefore, the biological matter and the cell were increasing their might from civilization to civilization. Because of this, the cell of a human who lived two thousand years ago has a thousand times less energy potential than the cell of a modern human.

Secondly, the changes in a human are caused by constantly changing conditions of the environment. Five thousand years ago, there was a different environment, and Earth and time were different. And clearly, a human has to fit in with time factor.

Time in each century carries its own new energy. And the imprint of time and its requirements affect absolutely everything. So, the latest human model must always correspond with a new time and the Higher beings' requirements.

The appearance of nations, nationalities, and their constant change has connections with the correction of work of a human model. While keeping its main construction, the organism's functions had to be changed in a way that while it remained of one race it was orientated toward work of a certain energy type (range), and while it was of another nation – toward a different type.

When Higher beings no longer needed the quality of energy that the nation produced, the latter was reconstructed into a different nation, or it died out gradually. Which goes to explain the constant changing of nations and nationalities, wherein the old are vanishing, and the new are resurfacing.

Nations originated because hierarchical Systems required the new types of energies that a human produced. And this is the third reason that has influenced the necessity to introduce constant changes in the form of the body's construction. The Hierarchical System needs for energy ranges were extending, and their assortment was changing too. In order for Higher beings to receive new types of energy, the construction of bio-machines, which is humans, took place.

Let me employ an example of how a new cell for the future race was created. Human cells decay due to exposure to strong Sun radiation. The sixth race [sixth civilization], though, needs to be able to sustain increased radiation and powerful energy.

In the fifth race [fifth civilization, our current one], increased sun activity led some cells to mutate; and in particular, a cancer growth started to form in all organs. "In all", because the cells, despite all of them being different in their functioning, have to work in a new regime with increased radiation and increased solar activity.

The entities from the medical* System took cells affected by cancer, with changed new energy in them, from a human, and implanted them into the new construction of a human. Then the research, observation and correction of its functions took place.

In this way, a previous bio-structure was rebuilt on the base of old mutating cells and placed into a new progressive state.

New cells responsible for producing immunity to increased radiation have reacted calmly toward the changes in the surrounding environment. And radiation doses that were deadly for a human in the 1950s have become a norm for 21st century generations, and it will definitely be a norm for the sixth race.

Thereby, a new cell that is not afraid of radiation was grown on the base of the old generation. And on this base, the future generation's immunity has been created.

Thus, new diseases originate in one generation, progress in the next, and disappear without a trace in the third (somewhat exaggerated), because in the third generation, in the way specified earlier, the immunity is produced. And, for sure, this does not happen by itself, but with the help of Celestial beings, who are watching over the diseases' progression and receiving new transformed cells on the diseases' base; then, following the principle of their cells, they build a new biological structure for humans which will not succumb to a disease of this type.

Therefore, the bio-structure of the human of sixth race will be built based on cancer cells from our fifth race. And thanks to this base, the new sixth race generation will not get sick with cancer diseases and will be able to tolerate easily and without effect an increased radiation on Earth. In the third millennium, radiation will increase to a much higher degree. Nevertheless, the new human organism will be prepared to receive it without causing any damage to itself and its usual operation. Thus, while former generations were struck down by tuberculosis and cholera, newer ones can simply forget about those diseases: the credit for this belongs not just to our doctors but to the Celestial medics who are invisible to us.

CONFORMITY BETWEEN A HUMAN'S MATERIAL SHELL [BODY] AND THE POTENTIAL OF HIS SOUL

The truth can be misunderstood and rejected when it is not understood; yet it will not become greater or lesser in the reality of its existence. The sages [wise men] have spoken repeatedly about it, and we reproduce their pronouncements in our interpretation. A human's disbelief obstructs his perception of truth, which comes from an unwillingness to understand it. The discrepancy between truth potentials and whoever is trying to understand it is not an imperfection of different potential comparisons, but the Level discrepancy between the potentials of truth and the one who is trying to understand it. How is it even possible for an individual with a little potential, which points at evolutionary young soul, to understand the truth with a great potential? Without a doubt, the truth will show itself to him as an incomprehensible. He is not even able to understand the theories of earthly scientists now, as they, in a light of their own significant development, have implemented the mighty potential of their ideas into their information. Every individual perceives only the truth that has same energy potential as theirs.

The above can be discussed further, as this subject is immense and unending; however, the subject being dealt with here is conformity.

The question is why do we think that underneath each existing concept there is a potential?

Let us start with the statement that all, that exists, is alive [living]. Even physical matter will not manifest its form of life if it is not a spiritual potential part of the soul. Any accumulations collected by the soul into the matrix are different energy types, which, together, create a soul's potential. The larger the accumulations of various energies are, the bigger the potential and might* of a soul is. Thus, the potential serves as the characteristics of strength and power [might] of the soul. It represents the Level of development of the form, as each Level, or each world, corresponds with a specific energy potential.

The above serves as evidence of the fact that each physical matter differs from other physical matter by the degree of its development.

The Higher being has told us that earthly physical matter is poorly organized because it is connected with the low potential of a human soul. This means that physical matter and the Soul are interconnected in their development and also interdependent.

Earthly matter cannot withstand the high potential of the soul, so it will only demolish; therefore, highly potential individuals from the middle of God's Hierarchy cannot be inside it, as they could incinerate and destroy the physical body. This points to the fact that natural suitability [conformity] must be present between physical matter and soul's energy potential that has to settle inside it. Only in that case a mutual progress of physical matter [body] and soul becomes possible.

If a soul with small potential is to be suited to a physical body that has achieved a sufficiently high Level in its development, the smaller potential of the soul will not be able to govern the higher potential of physical matter; thus, no progress can happen on either side.

The conformity between the physical matter and the soul inside it (souls from different worlds can also settle inside it) is kept within certain boundaries, so they (the soul and its material shells) reside in a harmonious parallel existence. And if we take the top borderline of the soul within this interval and the bottom borderline of physical matter, then said soul can govern many processes inside it, which a human is unable to do just yet.

In the worlds where physical matter and the soul have achieved a high Level of perfection, to which humans still need to grow and grow, the physical body is developed to such a degree that it is open to the soul; therefore, the soul manages and governs the body on the atomic and molecular levels in perfection. Individuals like this possess extraordinary abilities, but for them all this comes naturally.

The body of a human is not yet developed in conformity with the soul; therefore, even in highly potential individuals, located at the hundredth earth Level, not all qualities of extraordinary abilities are revealed. And because of this, making the body obey the soul is quite difficult.

Notwithstanding, there is a goal in front of humanity, and in front of other physical forms of life, to raise each other's Level mutually, as evolution progresses, until both can achieve the proper heights, which will unfold extraordinary properties in both. Physical matter, like the soul, has many unusual and mysterious abilities and qualities; yet, in order to reveal them further development is required.

THE ENERGY ASPECTS OF SOCIETY'S DEVELOPMENT

A human has always been lost in thoughts about how to live better and how to be happy. In order for the latter to become a reality, his own efforts are not enough; it is necessary for society to act in a certain way toward a private individual and not hinder his happiness.

It is common knowledge that a person cannot be happy in a society that does not match his ideals or perceptions of happiness. For example, if an individual thinks that only the wealthy can be happy, then he creates material wealth. However, society is wild [feral, primitive], and has its own goals such as starting wars, killing others, and destroying the habitat. In such a society, a rich person cannot be happy. He will worry constantly about his wealth.

Or, the situation could change. A rich individual ends up in very progressive society where people appreciate spiritual values and not material ones. In this case, he becomes like Pushkin* [a fictional character described by Russian novelist Nikolai Gogol, who obsessively collects everything he finds; a hoarder] who collects things which have no meaning to others, because everything this society has is different. Thus, this person could not be happy either.

These are examples of a mismatch between understanding personal and societal goals. Therefore, there must be a link connecting an individual and society. This could be any of the various spheres of human activities, such as politics, art, economics, science, and so on. These unite people from different societal backgrounds through the specific goals.

Joint goals and aspirations allow laws and rules of existence to be created for each separate member of society, which protect their interests. And only when a member finds support in his societal group, can he feel if not happy, then at least confident in tomorrow. Thus, the latter compels the private individual, who protects his own personal interests, to accept work for a common goal, and to not be in separation from others, but in solidarity.

Life, as we say, compels him to return to communal connections. But besides the human connections there are cosmic ones too, of whose existence he never suspected, though he was constantly revolving around them.

A human always has counted himself as a stand-alone unit, free from any responsibilities. But it turns out that his connections are expanding not only into society, but into the Cosmos. And the reason hides in a simple truth: everything in the world interacts with everything else, and definitely, with time.

In the first plan, there are always the goals of the Cosmos in accordance with the Higher beings' plans, which is first factor that impacts on humankind's life. The Higher beings subdue the life of humankind to their goals. And we can see in the examples of Sodom and Gomorrah, the annihilation of the Atlantis civilization, and present-day destructions on Earth what happens when their concept gets distorted. Floods, earthquakes, landslides, hurricanes, and other catastrophes are the result of Their actions, aiming to influence human behaviour, and to change it toward the direction they need.

The main thing to be seen here is that the distortion of normal connections between humankind and the Cosmos leads to a negative aftermath, first and foremost, for the human himself.

Humankind is linked with the Higher beings by one kind of bonds, and with its kindred by another kind. One of very important binding factors is time, as without it no bonds will work. Thus, the Higher beings' plans and time are two main factors that govern and create bonds. Everything else is derived from them.

The human body is a mechanism for the producing and transforming energy. A single human produces energy in a small volume, but the whole of humankind provides the Cosmos with a powerful outflow. The quality and quantity of this energy is regulated by individuals' personal programs and by the programs of nations and whole Earth.

The regulation of energies produced by a human through his personal program is explained in our other books many times, and that should be understood by now. This happens through the creation of various situations and also through an influence on feelings.

Society's programs are regulated through different levers [means] such as politics, economy, art, and so on.

As time passes, the Cosmos needs to receive different energies from humankind. Therefore, the Cosmos starts implementing different mechanisms into the human environment, which brings about a change on the inside of society from its previous work rhythm to a new one; thus, the production of old energies stops, and the production of new ones begins.

These short-term levers move society onto a new work regimen that includes ethics and morals, revolutions, reforms, and wars. Ethics and morals, as global mechanisms of influence, execute these levers after longer periods of time; however, they do everything to a superior standard of quality. Thanks to the rise of ethic and morals in society, it becomes possible to significantly improve the quality of energies produced for the Cosmos.

Energy of such high quality is impossible to produce with any other mechanism; although, a change of energy type can happen in the shorter term for a specific group of people. Usually, these are not huge areas of changes. In other words, revolution, war, reform, and so on, usually act as a strong driving force that shakes the whole society and breaks down the old, after which the new starts to be built. And it is not just a few individuals that will participate in this process, but many. Initially, the most important factor of these processes is that individuals receive general guidelines for new behaviour in new situations from Higher beings through their channels, and then secondary individuals will expand these guidelines to the rest of society.

Accordingly, the new mechanism gradually expands onto each private individual, changing their way of life and also their energy production.

The politics is a powerful lever that changes the main type of energy produced by a society. If Higher beings are in need of receiving cleaner energy, they implement a rigid regime such as slavery, dictatorship, serfdom, martial law, and so on. If other types of energies are required, calmer modes are implemented; for example, a system such as capitalism, socialism, or communism, and so on.

Naturally, the system and common rule dictate over all other sectors, such as the economy and art. One derives from another so interdependently and coherently [consistently], that there is no point really in talking about it. But here is a brief historical reminder.

If a dictator is in power, he will direct all funds available toward the development of the suppression apparatus. If a freethinker stands in power, he will direct the funds toward the development of science, rural farms, and manufacturing. If the ruler is a proud and greedy person who wants to secure a grip on a whole world, he will invade others' territories. These all are examples of the dependency of economy, art, science and such on politics and leadership.

Politics and economy are a regime which compel society to produce either positive or negative energies. Also, art and moral laws influence the production of energies of a different spectrum by human bio-machines; however, their influence is a mild one, as regulators of the energies' quality.

Art also has low and high energies, but both make corresponding souls to develop and to move in some definite direction. Correspondence [conformity] in this case consists in low art helping the progress of young souls that just started their development and does not influence those who already proceeded far enough on their evolutionary path, that is, average and advanced souls.

The art that is built on high energies, with high goals implemented in it, influences high souls in a beneficial way, resonating with them, and helping them to produce high frequency energies through the emotions and work of the astral shell [astral subtle body of emotions, feelings].

In a prosperous society, all art works toward positive energy production. And only when the society has degraded and outlived itself, does it start working for negative one. It becomes a testimony of the dying throes of this given regime, formation, and society.

The mechanism of producing energies is implemented in forms of human relationships, such as politics, economy, art, science, and social norms and rules.

When a newly created, strong society is just starting to develop, everything works clearly, and the predominance of positive energy production takes place. Then, the equilibrium state is reached, in which the quantity of positive energy produced by the society equals the amount of negative energy. After that, the downfall and prevalence in the production of negative energy by the society begins, which by increasing gradually, brings the society and formation into destruction.

Positive and negative energies are necessary for any civilized society in order to establish a common direction of movement toward the path outlined from Above.

Nevertheless, besides positive and negative energies, any society produces energies of different qualities, or different frequencies, creating a wide range of them. And all these energies are necessary in order to meet the needs of the Cosmos.

High and low frequencies are present in both positive and negative energies. They are necessary climbing steps in the general flow of evolution. By examining them, it is possible to determine the degree of development of any individual object and direction Of his path.

In order not to confuse negative energy with low, and positive energy with high, one must remember that in any negative energy flow there is an endless amount of both low and high frequencies. The same is true in a positive flow. And all of them are produced on the earth plane by humankind through interactions with one another. Various connections present themselves as subtle processes on the domestic and societal planes, expressed through human beings' various activities.

Two powerful flows of positive and negative energies are created on Earth by humankind, and then they are directed into the hierarchical Systems, where they continue their transformation on Levels of Hierarchy. There is a purpose to mentioning this, for a human to understand that he is not just leading a parasitic existence in the Cosmos;

but, as on any Level plane, he is the provider of a certain production (energy) for a higher plane.

Thus, all of the lower Levels on Earth, which are represented by minerals, plants, and animals, provide humankind with something useful. From each underlying Level humankind receives material produce such as rocks, which are used to build; and plants, which are used for food and the creation of a breathable atmosphere for human and animals, and so on.

Now the time has come for a human to find out the truth for himself, and as he does it becomes clear that he also serves as an intermediate link in the infinite chain of stages of existence. And each plane is based on an underlying level and receives certain kinds of energies from it; while producing other kinds [of energies] for the superior Level. Each level has its own ways and methods of energy production. On the human plane, these are common to our fields of activity. What we count as politics, economics and art are the processes of energy transformation and energy production, and at the same time, processes of soul perfection from a Cosmic point of view.

Our life, it turns out, is not as simple as it seemed to us previously. There is nothing in it that exists on its own. Everything participates in global processes of interexchange and is part of this process itself.

THE SPECIFICS OF SOUL PERFECTION AT THE TRANSITIONAL PERIOD FROM THE FIFTH TO SIXTH RACE

Let us take a look at the word of God where He speaks about the connection of a human structure with the physical world, its construction, and some changes in the principles of the structure's progress.

"The term logic, which pretends to be fundamental in its presentation of factors, is bringing an all-encompassing form of trinity in everything, into reality. From precision with regard to what is being said, comes the position of your initial stage of lifelong configurative* planes, with their building network being a numeral functionality with cybernetics as its ready function.

The calculation of the programmed installation source of a distributive nature is provided by the brain and spinal cord that govern and organise the previous functions' activity. The support of the apparatus described above assists in the configurative development of calculated constructions of an arbitrary nature, in which the leading value is assumed by a human Determinant.

While human nature undergoes this transformation the conflicting processes of youth and aging continue. The processes fit irregularly into the programmed and computed [calculated] functions, obstructing progress at the subtle planes and the development of shells and the structures attached to them.

The visible positions of human structures provide an instability in the construction of this given and chosen human apparatus type.

Over time, we are planning to remove old age and adolescence (up to the age of fourteen) from the programmed operations.

A human must be a continuous carrier of life situations with energy, which, because of the physical-type construction of his unchanging shells should not function to decrease or increase the programming, but potentially build up the energy-intensive saving ratio, which contains in itself the set of situations of planned and organizational qualities required from each Essential structure. These qualities are:

1. Responsibility to the goal that is set;
2. Obedience and respect to a superior;
3. Responsibility for the given words and promises;
4. Diligence.

Examples of the above qualities, when present in an individual, will lead them to be produced in other individuals, who will follow the main

Entity* that already has this different structure [with the above qualities], which has been perfected with time.

Environmental stability, which will prevail in the future, potentials to be produced that can be contained in the great energy capacity storage device. And the development of each individual unit will bring a potential advantage to their accelerated development, which will allow participation in the development of a whole structure of generations during only one physical lifetime. The development [of generations] will be conditioned by the guidance and training elders, who will be of the same age. "Elders" means they are superior according to earth time, but physically they are of the same age.

Since there will be no old age and no adolescence and everybody will be the same age, people will look like they are in their thirties, regardless of the years that will follow."

The information given from the Above that is built on a great deal of new terminology, introduces to humans entirely new concepts regarding the construction of the world and man.

The fundamental feature of the construction is in the trinity of all that is spiritualized. The trinity is in the souls of rocks and humans, and the creation of the world and humans is based on this trinity. This common feature allows everything dissimilar to be united in one functioning whole and in working for common Volume [plane of existence, macrocosm] in which it exists and develops.

However, the most important factor of this description is to underline that all these different structures are linked to one another with certain dependencies and functions, and they do not exist apart from one another.

Everything that resides in a specific volume [dimension, plane of existence] obeys its main functions and qualities. Therefore, any form, when it is being constructed, is linked with them not only in its physical, but also in its subtle, structure. In this relationship every form depends on the ancestral plane from which it comes, and for the human this plane is a physical world and its matter. The body of a human cannot be foreign to a given world; otherwise, it will not be able to interact with it.

The uniform qualities and building elements, which are ingrained into the composition of a body's physical matter and into the surrounding world, must work jointly; thus, they must possess many similar parameters for the units that constitute them (molecules, atoms).

Yet, physical matter always stays by a Level lower than the soul that is in it. And it is designed with the purpose of higher matter being able to govern lower matter; thus, the soul governs the body. At this time, this governance manifests itself to a weak degree; and because of that, it does not allow the unfolding of human abilities. Nevertheless, the governing part of the soul always controls the body and influences its acts.

This governance is not an unshakable constant. The program, implemented in the structure of a human, is engaged with an "upbringing" of the governing part, which means that the further development and perfection [of a human structure] goes through the governing part. By changing positive and negative qualities of his triune soul base, a human, by his own actions, influences changes in the qualities of the Governing part of his triune base.

The program is of a prime importance.

It dictates the scenarios of possible behaviour for a human according to his Level; and, by choosing these possibilities, he accumulates positive and negative qualities in himself which shape the Governing base of the soul.

At the same time, the choice that a human makes at the present time depends precisely on previous accumulations in the matrix, from which Governing part was formed in past lives. Thus, there is an interdependency of influences, whereby the Governing part influences actions, and the actions influence the Governing part. The finesse of their relationship consists in the choices a human makes in each situation and how the knowledge received is apprehended.

If we are to view the human body's form as a bio-structure that gets governed by soul, then it is possible to say that humans belong to a cybernetic device.

The soul's governing part is tied up with the brain's functions and the spinal cord which controls the physical substance of a body. For a human, it is hard to imagine this mechanism of transfer from the soul's Governing part into the body's Governing apparatus. In the same way, one who is not knowledgeable about technology will be incapable of comprehending the TV work principle.

Any action produced by a human is subject to calculation [estimating], meaning that any specific situation demands a certain energy expenditure from a human. Thus, when a program is outlined for the human, the maximum amount of energy an individual will need in each situation has been calculated, so that an individual will be able to endure these situations.

This computation [calculation] is based on the scenario that will demand the maximum energy expenditure from an individual. If an individual chooses the situations with minimal energy expenditure, he can possibly have some reserve for his future life, which is a positive thing, as we know that energy over-expenditure threatens life situations by adding complexity to them in the future, bringing a harsher fate.

Therefore, the Determinant of a human issues the planned amount of energy daily for the upcoming day and nighttime situations. The quality of energy is considered as well. Some situations use energy of one quality, and the others use energy of a different quality. And the Determinant is in charge of all that, or, to be exact, the Determinant and the program both regulate which energies must be produced by a human through his emotions, feelings, and situations, and which ones he can accumulate into his matrix at his given Level. Thus, everything is calculated according to the programmed scenarios.

One feature of the soul perfecting in the material shell is that a human is constantly given a feel of childhood and old age with the goal of schooling him [teaching life lessons]. Yet, sufficiently mature souls start a conflict with both, as childhood does not allow for a mature soul to aim right away toward the main goal at full speed; and old age, despite the soul having reached maximum strength and experience, concludes a human's opportunity for his best manifestation and further progress.

By successfully winning in apprehending something and perfecting some individual qualities, the soul loses time. Therefore, it starts a conflict with the body and with the stages, such as childhood and old age. By means of various reincarnations, the [mature] human souls have already undergone sufficient moral development; thus, old age, as a factor in teaching life lessons, has lost its former importance.

Higher [Celestial] designers, taking into consideration the soul's dissatisfaction because of this, are trying to implement the improved model of a human into the future race by removing childhood and old age, as it was indicated by us in the book "Secrets of the Higher worlds" (chapter "Gold race"). At the present time, these identified stages are slowing down the development of human subtle structures, preventing them from an intensive increase of their potential.

Childhood will be removed from the previous scenario of existence, where children spend much of their free time in vain. However, it should not be understood that a human will start his life as a grown up, in adult form, right away. The body will still grow from a toddler stage up to an adult stage; nevertheless, this process will accelerate.

This initial stage of the development, however, will be filled up with a different content, in which the situations will be directed more toward the soul's perfection in each human being. There will be no more wasted childhood. Life has to be filled with cognition and mastering something new, such as new forms of movement, or taking control over subtle energies or acquiring knowledge about subtle worlds, and so on. From working with crude [coarse] matter, the human will evolve more toward working with the subtle planes.

Due to the implementation of three and four development programs to the sixth race, the intensity of life situations will increase. All of this will allow accumulated qualities to contain more energy. Humans will begin to acquire various experiences rapidly, including organizational [organizing] ones, as every individual must learn how to lead, to govern, to plan; and of utmost important, to direct people who are subordinate to him onto the right path, regardless of whether they are his colleagues, his family, or any other society.

The goal of any governing individual is not to take pleasure in power and in people's submission, but to learn to take into consideration the common good. This means learning not just to provide monotonous work for an entrusted group of people, but to take great care of their comprehensive [widespread] development, promote abilities and aspirations to higher standards, satisfy and provide for their material needs in order to replenish their physical strength, set up the conditions for the creativeness, and fight against degradation.

All Levels in God's Hierarchy are based on the submission and governing of an underlying [lower] level by a superior [higher] level. Higher worlds build, plan and govern the underlying worlds.

Therefore, even at the current stage of the development of humankind, a need has risen for the development of its organizational skills. These skills do not just develop during one lifetime. When a human reaches the first Level of Hierarchy, they will be developed properly.

If five hundred years ago many qualities were not needed, now is the time to cultivate them in a human. And one can start cultivating now, beginning with his own family. The family is not given for a human to be comfortable in life, but to develop societal relationships and the ability to interact with the various age categories and character types in it. Thus, starting from that mini cell [family], it is crucial to develop a responsibility in yourself for any work that you have started, and for the destiny of each person that comes near you.

Higher beings establish the global goals which contain the setup of the whole worlds with a variety of life forms in them. And by looking at this goal it is possible to see the magnitude of their responsibility for all that is alive and for the correct orientation in their development.

Similarly, a human, in the course of his development, will grow from personal mini goals, like building a family and creating peace in it, toward the fulfilment of some grandiose goals. Thus, he shall start learning this right now. And through the family, God grants him this opportunity to master organizing, organizational skills and to develop a sense of responsibility.

Yet, as a human is located at a subordinate [lower] level, he is unable to understand and to appraise many things correctly; thus, he must not be arrogant, and he must know to acknowledge his improper actions and be willing to correct them. In order to understand the presence of mistakes, it is necessary to heed Superiors and to obey them unquestioningly, as superior experience has many benefits over inferior. Anything that is unnoticed by an inferior level human, will be noticed by a Superior. Therefore, it is very important to develop the qualities in oneself such as "obeying and respecting a Superior".

As a future organizer [coordinator], a human must get used to being responsible for all his promises and words spoken to his subordinates. Such a responsibility is not just discipline, it builds a human qualitatively. In himself, in his structure, and in the soul's Governing part consistent patterns must function, which later on will be governing him as the qualities of his character. In this relationship, a human develops his character throughout many of his lives and situations.

In particular, a quality of character such as diligence is developed by a human throughout his life. Nonetheless, some individuals think that to be excessively obedient is undignified; moreover, they feel that fulfilling the tasks given to them is a humiliation. Thus, they try to break away from under someone else's power so they can gain full independence.

However, this independence is an illusion. There are always superiors over an individual, and They direct his affairs not toward a sweet cloudless existence, but to where they deem appropriate.

In attempts to shy away from submission to someone, the individual avoids developing qualities, such as diligence, in himself. Yet, Higher beings place a special value and meaning on this particular quality. Thus, whoever avoids obeying others in fulfilling the assigned work (naturally, we are talking here about positive [righteous] actions and not those that lead to the Devil) will be compelled by Higher beings into developing diligence by means of harsh situations. In the worst case, one will be sent into a negative System, where no personal wishes are allowed, but only compliance with what is ordered from Above.

And here it is important to outline: the absence of qualities such as diligence and a compliance to orders that bring physical or moral damage to others, leads to Devil. That is to say that diligence must be wise, but not blind, for those who wish to be in God's Hierarchy. Thus, the qualities named by Higher beings, which must be developed, are very important to our [Celestial] Teachers.

When an individual takes a leading post and shows some traits of character named above, he becomes an example for his subordinates. Through imitation, subordinates develop the qualities Higher beings need; however, the constructions of individuals can undergo changes as human forms are constantly improved. Every effort will be made to account for failings by the fifth race and to have liquidated them in the sixth race.

This also will be done at the expense of implementing a more modernised human body construction and stabilised way of life. All will be directed toward accelerating the build-up of the soul's energy potential. By undergoing through three and four programs at the same time in one lifetime and by participating in an accelerated soul revolving cycle (they will reincarnate more often and stay for a shorter period in the subtle plane that that in fifth race), they will gain time in development. Thus, the perfecting of souls will accelerate substantially. This will be a leap forward.

A particularity of the sixth race's development is the consistent age of its society; in general, everyone will appear to be in the same age category that has stopped at the mark of 30-35 years old. The society will be composed of young and beautiful people, and old and middle-aged faces will disappear from view. Those who reach the age of 50 and above will continue to look like they are thirty years old.

In such a society, those of an older age who have undergone more reincarnations and accumulated a greater encapsulation of life experiences, compared to others, will lead. So, on the outside, people will look the same and will vary only by their inner qualities, accumulation of the matrix, and the soul's energy potential. Relationships will be completely new.

Full of life force, and not being destructed by old age and illness, the representatives of the sixth race will help close all the gaps which our fifth race allowed to open.

CHAPTER 3

THE PRINCIPLE OF THE INFLUENCE OF TV PROGRAMS ON HUMANS

We have already written that TV serves as a mechanism for the collection of energies that are produced by the human through his emotions (book "Revelations of Space," chapter 13). Now let us look at this subject in more detail in relation to the TV work principle and its interaction with human feelings.

The television broadcast is an ideal modification of the energy collection mechanism at the present time. It is built based on work with many ranges of the various types of energies. Additionally, it separates energies according to frequency, which facilitates their purposeful movement toward their egregors* in higher layers.

Divided or separated energies are easier to capture as they do not require additional processing. An example of undivided energies, for comparison, is a thought form*. In order to receive a specific type of energy from it, it must undergo additional processing.

Yet, how does TV work, and how does energies' collection and dispatch Upward, where they are gathered in special energy storage, occur?

There are various programs on the TV such as economics, politics, military, musical, and so on. The programs are constructed in such a way that elicits some kind of feelings and exhibition of emotions in humans. A human cannot remain completely indifferent toward what he sees. He always reacts in one way or another. Strictly speaking, he is watching something in order to feel something and to receive some impressions from the TV program. Thus, any indifference, or the absence of reaction to something, is only conditional [unconfirmed].

There are a few types of indifference that exist, such as the indifference of sadness (this is one type of energy), the indifference of pride (other type of energy), the indifference of cruelty, arrogance, or weakness, and so on. And all of them are different energy frequencies, not to mention the other feelings such as love, joy, hatred, inspiration, and so on. Therefore, regardless of what show a human is watching, he will always react to what he has seen, and he will do so according to the baggage of energies he has already accumulated during his past incarnations.

There are three types of interaction and reactions to what has been seen, such as acceptance by the soul, rejection, and, as was discussed by us above, indifference. In all three cases there are reactions occurring on the inside of a human, in response to which he produces a certain kind of energies that this show has been calculated for.

The action mechanism works in a way that when accepting to watch the entertaining show offered, the soul resonates with the energy range that this show was built on. The resonance strengthens an impulse, provides an emotional outburst; thus, feelings representing all the reaction types in a physical body, are starting to work on the astral shell.

If a person watches a movie in which cruelty, violence and rough scenes entertain him, then the energies of cruelty and violence will start to resonate with his soul. Supposedly, he had these energies in an insignificant quantity; however, when he is watching such films, and under the influence of resonance, his emotions engage in the work, and an energy processing mechanism is set in operation; so the soul gradually starts to build up negative qualities such as cruelty, desire to supress, to subdue others, and to impose his will on them.

If a soul does not like something, firstly, it starts to develop the same type of energy by accumulating a part of it in itself and by growing and anchoring a certain quality of a character. Secondly, a part of the human energies produced is thrown out of his organism boundaries and is captured by the TV screen. Thus, the TV is built from many cells, and each of them is calculated not only for the reproduction of images but for feedback from a human. The TV traps the energies of certain frequencies produced by the work of feelings.

Humans invented the TV with the single goal of having fun. Nevertheless, Celestial designers, when they sent the idea of TV's invention to the people, had a different goal in mind: to obtain the largest quantity of various energy types and their separation for a better distribution for energy storage.

Moreover, via TV, individual testing is possible, turning a human into a zombie; and other operations can also be performed. However, these goals emanate from different Systems, positive or negative, depending on the type of experiments they are working on, and on what they are trying to reveal in a human being. But the main goal is capturing [collecting] energies.

The TV is a capturer of energies. Usually, millions of spectators watch a movie and energy comes into the TV from each of them; so, if the movie displays cruelty and violence, it effectuates a powerful negative energy release of cruelty into the Cosmos as the result.

Nevertheless, by watching such a film, many can experience disgust toward the scene; in that case, an energy of the opposite quality will be developed, which the TV is collecting as well. Even in the same family, a few family members will develop the different types of energy from viewing the same movie. And all these energies will be perceived by the TV, get separated, grouped, and sent to an antenna from whence they will be directed further, into the Higher cosmos space Systems.

In the Cosmos, the already separated energies, will exit from millions of TVs. Every antenna has a dual purpose: it receives the waves with the reflection of one spectrum (which is a material range of frequencies) and emits a more subtle energies type in a different spectrum, produced by a human.

Let us view a scenario when a person watches a movie indifferently, and it seems that he does not enjoy it. However, because he is watching and sees the show, he is involving himself, voluntarily or involuntarily, in the process of producing and separating energies. The pleasure from low scenes or indifferent viewing provides the soul with negative quality energy. And only the rejection of them can develop positive energy.

Thus, in any case, energy collection takes place for every individual that watches the show.

The Nano sphere has totally different structure from what we can see. The earth, in its subtle constructions, is very complex in its build, which is inaccessible to our perception and comprehension. Therefore, when we are talking about energy capturers located around the planet and energy collectors dedicated to the collection of energies produced by people, we can only assume the constructions of the subtle plane, which are invisible to a human eye.

Before the invention of the radio and TV, these energy capturers had a complex construction, and they allowed inaccuracies in the collection and separation of energies. Radio and TV allowed for a step-by-step improvement in energy capturing by raising the frequencies separation quality, where low energy frequencies stay in the material layers and higher spectrum ones are allowed to go up.

As humankind had deviated from their mandatory development [progression] program by the end of twentieth century and started to produce large quantities low frequencies energies, the energy capturers, which were not calculated for such volume of filth, stopped working, and filth poured into the Universe. This is like a sewer blocked by faeces which have surfaced up the drain.

The process is the same for lower frequencies. Thus, humankind is 'to be corrected' from Above and to be brought up to the ethics and morals that will facilitate once again producing high (superior) and pure energy.

The radio works along the same principles; however, there is less feeling involved in the process, and the collection of energy and separation of it by frequencies is not as effective. All emotions and feelings come through the hearing apparatus only, so the spectrum of energies is inferior to that of the TV.

The colourful shows on the TV screen are capable of touching various feelings in a human's soul. The more subtle an individual's perception of the colour shades and his sensual perception is, the broader the spectrum of energy that will be produced by him.

Before radio and TV's creation, energy was produced by a human through participation in various situations and in response to his reactions to different scenes of nature. There were entertaining activities as well. Nevertheless, there was no such thing as a regulated mechanism of energy collection as is the case with radio and TV. Subtle energies were ejected in the surrounding environment after which they went into the energy collectors. However, with such a mechanism, a lot of energy was lost; and its quality was much lower.

TV, by composing programs, such as political, economic and humorous ones, plans the ejection of energy of a certain quality into the Cosmos. Love lyrics will cause human feelings to produce a certain energy spectrum, while a humorous or patriotic show will produce another, and so on. Thus, when shows are based on highly spiritual and moral norms, they encourage the production of high energies by people; and when based on low norms, the filth spreads into the Cosmos, so that the "faeces" of low [inferior] souls that poison near-Earth space compel the Hierarchical Systems to resort to extreme measures such as the destruction of people (by means of various cataclysms, accidents, wars, natural disasters, and so on).

TV shows which are built on high fundamentals of morals, ethics and religion are supposed to give the Cosmos a pure and luminous energy. Nonetheless, because people direct the shows toward the wrong stream, a negative effect is produced instead of positive one. Therefore, TV will gradually improve, and people will also find other ways to pass their time.

The new sixth race will base their lives on spiritual principles; thus, the need for base [inferior] and dirty shows and entertainments will disappear.

THE SOUL'S FAMILIARIZATION WITH THE PROGRAM OF FUTURE LIFE

Why does a human always like his appearance, regardless of the body type and shape he resides in? And if he were offered his neighbour's or his best friend's body, he would not agree, even if they were very beautiful and athletically built. One's own body, and face especially, are always beloved, even when some imperfections are present.

During reincarnations, the soul relocates from one body into another, and each of them in the current life appears to it as its own, beloved, and dear.

If a human were to be shown his past appearance in his past reincarnation, he would perceive it as foreign. And he would treat it with criticism, pointing out its defects and deficiencies. A past life body is seen as unattractive, and a human will show no interest in it.

At first sight, this is easy to explain: a human usually likes himself at the present moment of time, and all the past, being old, cannot be liked.

A present body is likable because the person gets used to it from the childhood, and the power of habit is equal to the power of love.

However, there is another reason. No doubt, there are many people who are unhappy with their appearance. Thus, the ability to have a sober look at themselves has been given to them specially, with an educational [lesson learning] purpose.

Love toward one's current body seems like a hypnotic influence of the program, which gives the command to love oneself and one's own body, so that one can take care of it and keep it groomed, clean and healthy; and this love has been removed from the people mentioned in the paragraph above.

People, who are not happy with their body or face, begin improving them using makeup, hairdos, sport and fashion. They develop an enhanced sense of an outer beauty. The purpose of which is, of course, different.

A human can be given an unpleasant appearance due to karmic reasons; for example, in the past life he made fun of someone's appearance; and in order to punish him he is being forced to experience negative looks and being laughed at by the others. So, when a person is not happy with their appearance, there are two reasons: either their bad appearance has been given to them with the purpose of paying off a karmic debt; or with the purpose of making an individual the creator of themself (even if it just on outside).

Thus, any ugly girl, if she desires, can make herself gorgeous.

But as general rule, people like themselves and they enjoy looking in the mirror, dressing up nicely, and taking care of their bodies. When a soul does not have the two reasons indicated above, then there is normal relationship between a given new life-new body and love toward this body. Yet, how is love attained? Is it that simple?

Prior to the soul entering the body of a child, it goes through preparation work which is an adaptation to new program. The soul gets familiar with its future program, and in a sense, it becomes aligned with the future program, events and forms. Thus, the majority of people will like their lives, and enjoy them. The other two categories described above will suffer and moan, working off their karma and their past debts.

The program definitely orientates the soul toward a certain form, within which it has to live, and also toward some individuals that are supposed to play a role in that person's destiny.

Thus, a person, sometimes, might feel sympathetic toward one individual and have ill feeling toward another, at first sight. There is a saying that first impression is the most accurate ones. This is because at this first meeting, there occurs the soul's "remembering" that this person might bring happiness or trouble in the future.

The soul often memorises program, not in the situations but in its impressions (by the way, it is helpful to add that low [level] individuals are not allowed to get to know their program. They receive a rigid fixation to love their body). While getting familiar with the program, the soul is finding out that in certain situations some individuals will bring happiness. Therefore, when the situation occurs, the soul, at an intuitive level, will recognize that one person who must bring happiness from the crowd; thus, soul feels a special disposition toward him.

Or, at first sight, somebody starts experiencing a strong antipathy toward an individual. This could also be connected with memory of the soul. Nevertheless, insufficiently developed souls forget just about everything, and in their connections, they rely on the opinion of environment.

Thereby, the soul's preliminary acquaintance with the program is given in order for it to develop intuition, to see through people who are connected with the program, and also for it to like its future dwelling. Yet, why does the soul get orientated to like these situations and life?

The soul could cross over from one world into another, in which the environment and forms of existence are different.

But even if it lived in the same world a hundred, two hundred, or five hundred years ago, it would experience the world in a new incarnation feeling estranged, because its past memory is connected to a totally different environment. Therefore, all that is around the soul will seem foreign.

If there were no preliminary orientation with a given world's forms, the soul would not be able to live in new world with its old concepts about forms.

In order for the soul to perceive the new as normal, a cipher-translator from old concepts into new ones, including the future body's form and appearance, is implemented into the program. The soul attunes to its new physical shell. Before its incarnation, the soul must start loving its future body, regardless of what shape it has; thus, this love toward the self is implemented into the program, so that the soul that rules this body can cherish it, take care of it, and fight for its safety, as the program must be carried on until the end.

When the soul incarnates into the body of black [African] man, it likes itself; and it also likes itself in body of Chinese or French, despite being one soul in different bodies. The soul can be directed into a parallel world, and into a form that is unusual for it; however, the soul must get used to it. Therefore, the soul of animal that transfers into a human form must change its appraisal criteria for the physical shell and its new lifestyle. And this is achieved through the program. Individuals that do not belong in the situations of the program are simply not noticed or are met with indifference by a human. Thus, acquaintance with the program plays an important part for the soul.

If the factor of satisfaction with one's own body were not implemented into the program, then everyone would believe that his neighbour or friend had a better body, and they would consider it better than their own; in this matter problems and violations in fulfilling the program would arise.

After death, when an obsolete body is not needed, the setting of "liking oneself" gets removed; therefore, on leaving the body, a soul feels total indifference or even disgust toward it. If, due to unforeseen circumstances, a soul leaves a body in the middle of the program, it continues feeling sympathy toward it. And this is the specifics of the influence of the program on the soul.

The "entry" into the program by high [superior] souls prior to birth includes getting to be familiar with the future events. After birth, the memory is disabled, but a general impression remains. Thus, many are happy with their lives and with everything in them, and they say: "If I was given another life, I would have lived it the same way," meaning that they cannot imagine anything better than their current existence. But, in any case, nobody will allow them to repeat their lives again. Nevertheless, the fact that an individual likes his life and does not want for it to end is based on a preliminary acquaintance with the future program.

Naturally, not everything about the program is revealed, and the acquaintance occurs within the permitted boundaries; otherwise, no perfection of soul can happen.

After birth in a body, the attuning of soul toward the specific objects and toward oneself takes place. The soul adopts new concepts and connections, mastering the control and ownership of its material body. A subtle soul, as an energy substance, has difficulty in learning to control coarse matter; thus, for the child to master his body movements is a very long and hard process taking up to three or four years.

Yet, let us ask the question. Why do Celestial Teachers put such an emphasis on caring and paying attention to a physical body, and why are they teaching us to love it?

It is connected with the fulfilment of program by a human. The individual must fulfil it, no matter what.

If a human depreciates his body and does not look after his health by disregarding the norms of hygiene or puts himself in high-risk situations by getting into accidents; then he survives only because of the intensified work of his Determinant [Celestial Teacher, Guardian Angel].

A human cannot even imagine how much energy and life force his Teacher must spend in order to rejuvenate his body constantly (and even restore it with much more effort after the accident, so it can allow the program to be completed).

Determinant must make sure that a human is in such a state that allows his normal working capacity and the fulfilment of goals, given to him from Above.

If a person has neglected his hygiene or been reckless, putting himself at risk deliberately and, as the result, has harmed his health, it is his Determinant's responsibility to bounce him back to health and to cure. And he spends lots of strength, time and energy to achieve this.

Often, the work of the doctors is not enough. Determinant makes sure that his pupil delivered to the hospital in a timely manner, so that the soul will not leave prematurely before receiving help; he also makes sure that the sought-for, qualified doctor looks at him and administers the correct treatment, and so on. Thus, from the subtle world, the Determinant has to organize the work and make sure to direct the necessary people to his pupil.

When something unplanned happens, the Determinant has lots of work. And this is only because a human must fulfil his program until its appropriate end, main or optional [choices in the program]. If, by accident, he should die (when the body is so damaged that it is impossible to stay alive), then people who are linked with the deceased by their programs develop inconsistencies within their programs.

Such people find themselves in a dead end, from where they are unable to leave, getting lost in the events; and they do not know how to find a solution for the problem. Thus, there is a possibility that they will be unable to fulfil their personal programs; therefore, they will accumulate energy debts. The programs that are unfulfilled by a human can annul the other big tasks in the Cosmos, as everything is interconnected and intertwined.

Thereby, Celestial Teachers appeal to humans to respect their bodies, to take care of them, to abide all means of hygiene, and to practice all kinds of exercises.

If a person has enough comprehension to take care of himself, or, according to the plan of his program, he loves himself, then the Determinant has easier time working with said pupil, and he does not have to overrun the energy resources. Besides, with a good pupil, the Determinant has more free time for himself, and accordingly for his work in the subtle plane.

Only a desire for his pupil to fulfil his task makes the Determinant work to assist our health. And often the person does not even understand how close he was near death as the result of some improper actions; and only due to the Determinant's efforts, was he able to avoid the threat. Thus, for example, a person with an unhealthy heart can live up to seventy years old, and a person with healthy heart can die from a heart attack or cardiac arrest.

In the first case, the person with an unhealthy heart had to fulfil his program that was stretched for seventy years, so even if this person has damaged his heart with overwork or stress, the Determinant will constantly help him to recover.

In the second case, the person has turned onto wrong path, so even though his heart is healthy the Determinant has stopped him, causing a heart attack. The program ran into a dead end, so if not stopped, degradation would come next.

There could also be an illness that was written into the program. In this case, the Determinant must watch its course, so it does not cross the boundaries, but stays in a chronic form, without ending life.

The same is true for some risk situations. If they are written into the person's program, and the person must live until old age, the Determinant then has to watch that these situations do not become extreme (for example, in a stuntman, an athlete, or a soldier).

It is very important to teach a human to love his body and promote the correct work of his organism, so as to prevent illnesses, to maintain physical endurance, and to avoid unnecessary risks and such. When a person is able to regulate his normal condition and his health, the Determinant's work with his pupil becomes much easier.

The duty of each Determinant is to provide the necessary conditions for the fulfilment of program by his pupil. The duty of each pupil is to fulfil his program with a maximum return of energy to his Teacher.

THE ROLE OF INFORMATION IN SHELL DEVELOPMENT

There is lots of knowledge around a human, but not from all knowledge he is able to receive the information for himself, and neither has he learnt to read and decrypt. Usually, the comprehensibility of the information depends on the individual's level of the development; and the higher the Level, the more information he can comprehend from everything around him.

This given ability expands with the individual's progression, as a better developed soul has a larger volume of past concepts which allows them to be comprehended much more within the new information.

The acquiring of knowledge by humans is not a purposeless occupation, as they usually think. Everything goes into the spiritual luggage of the soul. The physical brain is a partial memory of present life. A human's past memory is multileveled and tied up with his subtle shell's accumulations in the matrix. Yet, in this case we will talk only about the subtle shells, or energy bodies.

The subtle shells of a human have their own memory. All seven energy bodies are built hierarchically. Each shell represents a certain developmental Level, as the energy body functions only with a particular energy range. Thus, it is possible to say that fifth race humans have developed in themselves seven Levels, in which the physical body is the lowest and spiritual is the highest. Thereby, a human has a Levelled structure, just like everything else.

Each level, in its turn, also has a certain structure that falls into the same hierarchy, or order. In the same way, for example, organs in the material body are situated according to hierarchical dependency as we wrote before. And the more perfected [accomplished] a human's soul is, the more subtle shells, or energy bodies, he will have.

Each shell accumulates information of a specific quality. In the shells, there is a mechanism of energies of a certain range that processes and redistributes them onwards through different shells, up to the matrix.

If mental energy [thinking] needs to be processed, the astral energy body [body of emotions] will not be involved in the work only in a case when thinking is solely connected with calculations. In all other cases, thinking is coloured by feeling; therefore, the energy redistributes from the mental shell into the astral shell, and into the physical shell and back, so that the energy goes back and forth. When the energies of the astral plane are developing, firstly they originate in a physical body, and become more refined for the astral shell [becoming more subtle when entering the astral plane].

Only the energies of fine qualities enter the matrix. If the shell does not produce those, then nothing comes into the matrix. Everything depends on the work of the soul. The more qualitatively it works, the more accumulations from the shells will enter the matrix. Every shell sends its own quality to the matrix, but only one that has already reached normative magnitude. A human could live his entire life without getting anything into his matrix from the astral or mental shells, and this is because they have not reached the required quality.

A human must engage the highest mechanisms in himself in order to create accumulations in his matrix. And he will be returned into life many times for that, so that the matrix can finally become filled with the energies of the earthly plane for the human to be able to climb higher. And in this perfection [enhancement], his shells play the main role by connecting him with this given [present] world and with the various ranges of its energies.

In same way, a physical body has its own energy processing mechanisms, represented in the form of organs. And accumulations in a physical body are characterized by the body and forms growth and their constant change.

Each shell is distinct and does not look like any other in its structure and in its principles of functioning. And this is related to the types of energies used in work. Thus, crude work with stone demands one type of technology, plastic-another, and wood-yet another.

The technology process is determined by the quality of the material and the goal of the processing. Just as in the energy bodies, the quality of energies with which they work and the goal of energy processing, determines the structure of the technological process that works in each energy body.

The shells collect certain accumulations. But any accumulated energy is an information carrier. Thus, accumulations form a memory of the energy body.

The information must correspond with Level of the development; otherwise, it will lose its momentum as a force that supports the soul's progression.

In development, an individual moves from simple to complex, and from coarse energies toward fine ones. That is to say that work with energies goes from the lowest energy potential to the highest. Therefore, an individual often has difficulty comprehending some new information, as his low potential is unable to grasp a potential that surpasses him. And only systematic work and persistence help him to move forward in the direction needed for his development.

Memory of the past is different in each and every energy body, depending on the type of energy from which they were formed; as different energy levels have their own qualitative accumulations, according to their order.

Different qualitative accumulations correspond with different information. The astral shell, in which the mechanisms that are working with feelings are located, processes [converts] and accumulates the energies of the astral plane. The mental shell has a totally different mechanism of conversion [processing], as it works with a completely different type of energies.

Comparing the difference in the working of astral and mental shells, human can judge how differently they are made, and the accumulations in one do not correspond qualitatively with the other, and this is also true of the type of energies accumulated. And the same applies to all other energy bodies.

Each energy body has its own thinking. Many people of a non-intellectual type think not with their mental shell [mind, intellect, brain], but with their astral one [emotions]. This is a primitive, common way of thinking. But in order for mental shell to work, one must first learn to think with one's astral shell.

When energies in low individual move from the causal plane shell into the astral shell, they pass throughout the mental body as through an empty space. Thus, the energy passes through the mental body without including it in the work, as the mental body is designed for work with a greater potential. Primitive actions are built on the astral energy body's thinking work.

Obviously, for this reason, the memory of these shells will carry different information that is not alike. Precisely, the different types of energies give different information.

A human's character is the sum of accumulated energies in all his energy bodies. His character depends on exactly what he has accumulated: the type of information and set of energies. Since all accumulations are [constantly] changing, his character does not possess a stable and consistent quality, and it changes as his personality develops.

Scientists have established that DNA contains a human's physical body development program and has ways in which hereditary traits influence the formation of a person's character. And precisely, that is why alcoholic parents give birth to future child-alcoholics; artists are born into families of artists; and in a scientist's family there are future PhDs.

However, the influence of DNA on character and behaviour decides only ten percent. Everything else is the soul, its matrix, and the latter's energy accumulations. And the accumulations of all shells combined add ten percent of the qualities accumulated in them toward human character.

The components of human character:

All subtle shells (10%) + DNA (10%) + matrix of the soul (80%) = character

A belief that similar habits, inclinations, or talents are to be found in families and these will be passed down through heritance and genes, does not reflect truth. These families are formed purposely, but not with the goal of creating precisely through DNA or genetic code a repeat of spiritual hereditary traits. Family clans are formed artificially by choosing certain souls. Low souls are sent into low families, and talented ones are sent into high families. The reason for this is to develop certain inclinations in the soul.

A child's soul in a family of musicians must accumulate certain qualities which the soul is missing. The child may not necessary become a professional. He just gathers the energies he is meant to. Alternatively, he might become some pop star, depending on his program's goal.

It is necessary to remember that some families are carriers of negative energies; therefore, the souls of individuals which have a right of choice are sent to them. They can take a negative path (become thieves, killers), or be devoted to sport or the army, producing qualities of a different type.

In order for a human to continue an ancestral succession, his inclination for something is not enough. It is necessary to have the corresponding program (such as a painter, a scientist, etc.). Sometimes, a low soul is sent into a creative family because it has a Karmic debt. This could be tied up with the energy structure of this family, and/or with the purpose of supporting the balance of positive and negative energies with which this family works. Thus, the DNA carries in itself only a part of some hereditary features responsible for forming a human's personal qualities.

Nevertheless, in the ancestral clan there is something else that exists, which is matter that forms the human body: either lower organized matter or highly organized physical matter (low and high organized matter is assumed only in relation to a given stage of development). A low soul moves into low matter; or to be exact, into a place specially formed for it inside the mother's womb of a low energy type body.

The low soul will demand low components from food in order to build its physical shell. Thus, the mother will have cravings to smoke, to eat salty or spicy food. One such woman, for example, liked to smell exhaust gas during her pregnancy. This indicates that the mother will give birth to a child who has a low developmental Level, in other words, a young evolutionary soul with the attributes of vice.

All higher energy components will be rejected by such a soul, being ejected from the mother's body as waste, as higher energies cannot be joined with a lower Level. A low soul cannot use the high energy components for building its physical body, as it has not acquired the degree of a certain potential necessary to be able to connect it with the energies of high potential. Such a soul does not have in-between structures able to provide an additional intermediate [medial] potential. Souls that have an average potential already, are able to attract high components, as they have not skipped a stage of their development [have consecutive development progression].

Needless to say, the previously mentioned is achieved through calculations. Higher beings determine the potential of the soul that is being sent out and the components which it needs for structuring its body; and also, the components that must be left out because of their potential, which is higher. Everything is achieved through calculations and then it is implemented into the body's construction program. Higher beings, moreover, have special methods of building the body depending on the implemented soul's potential; therefore, for Them to make such calculations is not difficult. It is a standard procedure. A human only sees the outside of the events hidden from his comprehension.

If a future mother is observed to be having strange habits such as being increasingly demanding toward her own cleanness and experiencing a disgust toward filth, then such "strangeness" can be connected with the fact that she might be giving birth to a child with a high soul. Such a soul, existing in Higher world, where is clean and bright, will demand from its mother certain conditions to which it was accustomed. And the body of such a child will be built from different components. We are not talking about completely different, but partially so, as human Levels do not vary much from one another in order to have a completely different quality of their physique. More often, the components are interspersed, so there are high and low components present, as in general, souls are average.

As the chemical composition of the body's physical matter depends on the type of the soul; high and low souls are found to have a qualitative difference in their physical matters that compose their bodies. It can be insignificant, but it can be seen. The chemical composition of high spiritual and low spiritual people contains differences. However, scientists have just started to discover this by finding components in the blood of negative individuals that are not present in the blood of positive individuals. Further research in this direction may bring many more discoveries about humans. Nevertheless, such discoveries might not even take place, as the current physical shell has outlived itself and will be replaced by a new one. The sixth race will have a physical body built from new bio-matter that has different qualities.

A further explanation about the outer form and subtle human shells was provided by the Hierarch of "Union"*.

"Today we will talk about vertebrate samples. They presented themselves as a new evolutionary branch called the vertebrate group, which was the best way to represent them as all kinds of cosmic equivalents, gathered together as one unit.

This one unit differs due to its focus on the psychological and evolutionary plane especially. This means that one or another kind of vertebrate has the same life focus [direction].

In order to get to know yourself, you must start getting to know your physical body first, and then reach toward the subtle planes. Despite the qualities of the latter becoming dulled [less obvious], every shell has a colossal exit into space. What that means is that every energy body has its own exit or path into its parallel world.

Each energy body is able to pass energy Higher up, thanks to such an exit.

By knowing how to use their own shells, humans would be able to live freely and perceive all seven worlds, situated on Earth, at the same time. The presence of parallel worlds speaks of the multiplicity of life planes, even on your planet.

Humans have not yet learnt to perceive all worlds, though some have attempted to access one or two. When a human has tried to inhabit them, his physical body has not allowed him. As it turns out, there is very high dependency on physical matter and physical appearance. These two factors will never allow him to travel freely into the parallel planes, as firstly, one can only exit into a subspace. The connection with the physical body will not allow him to proceed further; thus, the true world, into which he exits, will be hidden from his consciousness. However, by working on himself, a human can achieve much more.

The current human structure, however, is convenient for Our goals. Thanks to a special tuning, all bodies can be joined together, and, at the same time, their insularity can be preserved. This effect gives us an opportunity to receive particular energy types from humans from each of their energy bodies, which are processed [transformed] into coarser forms than the form initially given [to him] by Us. Thus, prior to entering into energy storage, these energies undergo cleansing. From there, We take them for the construction [creation] of new forms."

Which group of vertebrates does the Hierarch speak about and why does He isolate them into a separate, special group?

It turns out, the vertebrate group belongs not only to Earth, but to our entire physical Universe. There are all kinds of various life forms in it, the majority of them having an amorphous or solid state, or something that remains in a gaseous state for a human. Many forms of life exist, yet humans have no idea about some of them.

Nevertheless, the creation of vertebrates has had special significance for the material [physical] plane. The bones, as a solid base, made it possible to create special types of movements in a material [physical] environment (walking, swimming, flying-for birds), and to create the variety of forms themselves, not only on our planet, but on the other material [physical] planets, so that the vertebrate group has become a special branch of development in the Cosmos. Also, many aliens belong to the vertebrates, though they are still differentiated from a human. Thus, the underlying idea of construction is preserved and allows many forms to be combined in order to comprehend themselves, starting from what is visible and going toward what is invisible.

However, not all aliens possess such forms, as the majority of them belong to a subtle plane, where there are many more of them than on the material plane. A human mistakenly thinks that all sentient beings in the Cosmos would be exactly as himself. The amount of those exactly like human is limited. Even though there are some vertebrates, their outer appearance differs greatly from a human form.

The presence of coarse matter attests to the presence of subtle shells in aliens because an intermediate state must exist between coarse matter and a soul; thus, the preservation of a levelled structure is necessary.

The number of subtle shells in aliens depends on the degree of their development. Needless to say, the more highly developed the aliens are, the higher the number of energy bodies they possess. Since it is not humans who are flying to them, but they who are flying to humans, it seems natural to guess that they have excelled humans in evolution; therefore, it can be concluded that they have many more shells [subtle shells; energy bodies] than a human.

Nonetheless, a similarity of forms assumes a similarity in the methods of studying them. Therefore, obviously, in studying themselves, they went down the same path that we did. In regard to humans, it turned out that each of their shells is constructed in such a way as to have an exit into a corresponding parallel world of Earth. This fact opens up a monumental opportunity for the shell to learn about this world. Astral shells exit into the astral space of Earth, mental shells into mental space, and so on. Volumes that have homogeneous energy types connect. This allows Higher beings to better collect human-produced energies and store them in special energy storages. That is to say when a human produces energy of the astral plane by means of working with his emotions and feelings, a part of it enters his shell, and the other part, while going precisely through the Earth's astral plane and its [astral plane's] channels, is headed into its own energy storage.

Previously, a human has understood this process as an ascension of vapour from the Earth's water surface upward. The vapour collects into the clouds as it passes through the air, and the energy, as he thought, is being collected into the egregore [a collective intelligence, group mind] which did not have a specific structure. But now we know that astral energy ends up in the worlds with the frequency that corresponds to it first; and the identity of the energies and the specific structure of astral plane does not allow them to disperse all over the world; instead, they go to the place where they must be, such as the energy storage, where they are situated according to their frequencies, and in an ascending manner.

Because a human usually pollutes the energies he emits, they undergo a mandatory cleansing before arriving to the place they must gather at. The purification of energies occurs in the subtle worlds, with each of them having their own technology. Higher beings use only the purified energies for their needs.

A human does not know how to use his own energy bodies as of yet; for they can open up the opportunity for him to exit into seven parallel worlds of Earth, to get to know them and to learn about them. He can connect with the planet's astral plane through his astral shell [astral body] and with the planet's causal plane through his personal causal shell, and so on, accordingly. However, he must have the knowledge to do it, and he must study this. The knowledge of these worlds will support the perfection of the soul. Nonetheless, the human must not be moved by curiosity, or by shallow knowledge, but by the desire to undertake a serious, comprehensive study of the worlds. Through their study and by studying himself, the perfection of the soul takes place.

Part 2

CHAPTER 4

DIALOGUES WITH HIGHER BEINGS

In this part of the book I would like to present God's appeal to the contactees [channellers, people who receive messages from Above], and to the ordinary people; and also His first conversations explaining Higher worlds, along with His hopes for humankind, as well as the answers the Hierarchs have given to some of our questions. Here is the information from the very first contacts, while we were establishing the connection.

Before one can receive the Laws, God teaches how to listen to Him and how to convert His concepts into the right words. By means of the Divine Word, God tries to bring the concepts and goals that Higher Beings live by into the hearts of everyone, so that those who wish can move forward with Them.

Nevertheless, the path to Above lies only through a correct understanding of truths. Each truth that is perceived correctly and not distorted with a primitive egoistic consciousness fills the matrix with new and noble energies and elevates souls into the worlds of God. Therefore, every word and all information sent by God and his helpers contains in itself a priceless gift of glorifying the individual, but not in a low [primitive] understanding of this expression, but in a high [noble] one; thus helping to elevate [to perfect] each soul that would like to understand them and to move up the steps of the evolutionary ladder into the Higher spheres [dimensions].

And for this matter, all of God's words and His information, as well as information of the Higher Hierarchs, is a priceless gift for humans, because Levels communicating with us are way above first Level of [His] Hierarchy. Thus, we called Their information "pearls of the Higher truths" or life treasures, which God and His Hierarchy gift to a man, and which can be developed further and exert a beneficial influence on those who gather them in their souls.

"Pearls of the Higher truths" is the precious essence of each God's revelations that unlocks the secrets of Higher [Divine] existence only to a loving and trusting heart; thus, preparing a human for this existence through the perfecting of his soul. Therefore, we preserve any word of God and His Hierarchy as a great relic sent, and we want for every human to see the fiery scrolls of Their Thoughts, converted into words, and not just the combinations of words or difficult phrases.

God spoke to us through fire. Therefore (I am addressing history of receiving "The Laws of the Universe"), before receiving them, we had to move into a different house, which was located by the swamp, and on the water. Water is a perfect energy transmitter.

If we had stayed at our previous home, as we were told, the ground would have cracked under us (the other contactees from our group had predicted this as well). So, in order for this not to happen, we had no choice but to relocate to the house built on a more secure pile foundation. We had water in the basement constantly, as the ground waters stood high. Nevertheless, this allowed throwing the energy surplus during the contacts [channelling] to be thrown into the water, and then to be evenly distributed through underground water arrays.

Energy was arriving, and we felt it. Our main contactee [channeller], Seklitova, L, despite the cooling devices installed in her subtle constructions, as was explained by our Celestial Teachers, burnt her face in the process of receiving God's Laws; and she had to recuperate herself two years after that. She burned her face because she received the Divine energy through her head, via the impulse ring.

During my interpretation of the Laws, despite the energy coming having weakened, I still felt it burning inside me with an obscure cold fire. My throat, where the chakra of creativity is located, was burning. The heat became so intense at times, that I had to drink cold water or to turn on a fan. Some laws were so energy-rich [highly saturated with energy] that I felt overblown with energy. I felt that if I were to exhale, the fire would have come out of my mouth like from the dragon in a fairy tale.

These were our sensations during the writing of the Laws. Thereby, through each word, the Divine [Heavenly] energy was entering into us. And despite the books being printed in typography, and their potential being decreased (as this is a different mean of giving the information); it was still maintained in a way that was acceptable for a human, without being burnt, but filling his soul with the Divine fire. Thus, it is very important to comprehend and to absorb each word of God into the soul. The process of the soul's transformation occurs by comprehending its inner meaning and carrying out deeds that are worthy of God.

And now lets us refer specifically to the texts passed by God to Seklitova, L. A. during her first tuning contacts, which were preparing her to accept the Laws of the Universe.

"I will speak through you to the people who do not know and who do not believe.

My phenomenon is not a mystery. I never involve anyone in my plans, I just come; and who can see – will see Me, but the blind will not understand this phenomenon. I am coming to talk with people about what they have not been taught.

Let them trust me and comprehend My essence that was always open to them, with their mind. However, they did not hear Me.

Now you will cater to their souls that I must convince them, and I must change their minds and correct their actions. Now and presently, they will undergo the last correction on their way to Me.

I am saying that from their hearts their cleansing will begin. The man stays blind. He does not see Me and does not see and does not want to see his mistakes, revelling in indifference. I am giving them information, so they can see light.

The information that will be given to you will pass through diverse deciphering [decoding, transcript]: this is complex mathematics, physics, electronics, and many other sciences too. I will combine many things in you. You came to help Me to correct the world on Earth and to recode [restructure, reprogram] it. And no one will stop Me on My way of achieving My plans (*means those who do not accept anything new*).

There are many places on Earth from whence the recoding can be controlled. This recoding is necessary to me, and you must fulfil it.

Nonetheless, nothing is being built as smoothly as I had expected. And nothing is being done in a way that I wanted. However, great events are coming, and all My plans will be accomplished."

When the memory of the past is turned off and the goal is not conveyed to a human, there is no way to predict how his soul will behave. Thus, at the present moment of permissive freedom, many have acted against God's wishes; as they have started to chase material wealth, titles and to seek glorification from others.

When memory is unplugged and there are many low* [inferior] subjects around, who only pursue their petty and personal goals to satisfy their lust, animal instincts and other lowest desires, it is hard for the soul in such environment to determine what is important in life and should be desired, what is low [inferior] and what is high [superior, honourable]; what one should run from and what one should strive to get closer to with all one's strength.

The soul's qualities are revealed greatly in such environment (note I did not say "human's," but the "soul's"), as the soul is always bigger than just a human himself.

If a soul* is strong and without flaws, it will strive rigorously to achieve a Higher goal, by dismissing all that is inferior and the provocations of [from] negative Systems. If there are flaws, even the insignificant ones, they will always reveal themselves during the corresponding circumstances, and the soul will deviate away left and right from the High [Divine], using a variety of excuses.

Thus, God reminds each human of his main goals again. Everyone has shallow [petty] goals, but there is only one main goal for the whole humankind. God speaks about it:

"The main goal of a human life is unification with Higher beings and achieving a high level of spirituality with the help of Our knowledge.

The utmost importance for them is the comprehension of information which We sent. They must achieve what has not been reached, mentioned, or founded. The goal of life is in comprehending Our tasks. Otherwise, they will not walk the path that We have strived to lead them along all their earthly lives.

People, please think again one more time! And let the eyes open of those who do not know and are unable to come across to you, or to get to know Our information because of their remote location.

Those who are far away will gather by the fire and will warm up their hearts with Our fire. And this will be coming soon. The fire, started by Us, will burn, light up, and guide people who wish to go further and further. With that, all who are faithless and mindless [ignorant] will fall away and burn, so Earth will be cleansed out. And there will be much relief then for the "Union" *.

Those who have strong spirits, once they become touched by the noble fire, will rise up and grow, and they will lead their comrades after them. And there will be the pupils, and the pupils of pupils. And this is how it will be because I command it."

Later on, He spoke with more complexity about the goal of the human. As soon as we adopted [mastered; digested] his information, his syllables [phraseology] became more complicated.

"There is a new order for human actions during the progression of the soul. He must be guided by purposeful achievement of a final result for some goal that belongs to a corresponding developmental Level of Earth.

The achievement of a goal allows the potential of thoughts to increase and a tendency of the hierarchical, situated on a Levelled plane, to multiply which will lead the potential of your thoughts onto the path of self-improvement, as it gives birth to increased composure [control] over events, or, over the superficial reproduction of one or another kind of configurative approaches to actions.

All this will lead directly to a dependency on the greater potential of technical regressions, which is a necessary action for the reproduction of qualitative indicators of certain potentials in you.

Returning to the same action several times from different positions that in appearance positively look alike in relation to the functioning subject, is not welcomed by the Laws of the Cosmos.

Thereby, a goal that has not been achieved should not obstruct the way but be transformed into a potentially new vibration of a specific image.

In other words, you either achieve it right away or you transform it into a new image, into a new form, which gives you the opportunity of not stopping your development. A stop leads toward a steady degradation of an apparatus. Thus, a new form leads toward a new perfection, physical and spiritual, which is proportional.

To achieve a solitary [single] goal, on average, a human has up to six months in earth time reckoning."

In one of his contacts, God touched on the question about the descent of mighty energies to Earth. This is, precisely, the reason fires start in different corners of Earth that erase forests and destroy settlements. The same energies influence humans, impacting their different Levels of development differently. Below is how God started one of his contacts with Larisa Seklitova and us:

"From the time when I was with you at Our place (*meaning before our incarnation on Earth*)*****, **We were thinking of how to turn the face of humankind to Us, toward the spiritual, not the earthly. However, We have not considered how many people will become decoded from such a turn. The psyche of people constantly deviates toward undesirable directions for Us. Thus, many defective souls [souls with flaws] were revealed by tests and understanding of Our information.**

Nonetheless, nobody and nothing will obstruct My intentions. My plans are grandiose.

A human must understand a most crucial point. I destroy so I can create. And I never destroy anything in vain.

In order to keep a large organism orderly, the energy and system of its regularity [order] is required. If there is no order, then its opposite will appear: chaos. Ninety percent of what was planned by Me is chaos.

Humankind was given opportunities for correction on several occasions but did not use them. Thus, many souls will be sent to be melted down. Human souls for whom destruction have not been planned will exist in a new human appearance. These will be the people of the new epoch, a new race.

And the immense energy that We are descending to Earth will now be increased threefold.
Get ready, you will feel hot. The energy will help the planet and pure souls to climb up to the superior [higher] Level. This is a starting energy in order to go Up [Above].

At the same time, this energy will destroy those misguided souls embedded in sin. Thus, a great pestilence will begin on Earth. The cleansing is happening at great speed.

And again, for the last time, I am stretching out My hand to those who desire to be saved. And he, who is able to see, will see Me in new guise, but those with blind souls will hold onto the sinking ark.

And I want to say one more thing: From the great potential of descending energy, abilities are unfolding in weak bodies, but not for a long. This is destroying them. They either lose their minds or quickly die.

Naturally, the descending of great energy will introduce new diseases; however, they will only impact weak powers. Those with high power and a pure spirit should not fear. What is death for the low [inferior] is life for the high [superior]; and what is good for the low is death for the high. This must always be remembered."

In this text, everything is crystal clear. God expresses His disappointment with human behaviour. Many times He has given people chances for correction [to be better], but only one in a thousand is using this chance. The rest are continuing to behave immorally and dirtily, as always. Moreover, they do not see the immorality of their actions. Everyone thinks he is a saint; when, however, he reaches persistently into the pocket of another [person].

It has to be mentioned that the majority of people, living on Earth nowadays, are those who undergo through life and death test. Memory of the past is closed, and the soul is sent to life. How it will behave in the new conditions, with freedom of behaviour and thought? Where will it reach out to and how many points will it score in the life situations given to it?

Everything is thrown onto the weighing scales. Nonetheless, the human remains blind. He thinks that if everything is permitted, then he can take away from his fellow creatures, and he can indulge his low instincts, as freedom bestows an aureole of "trendiness" to them. It is modern to use the word "sex" and to regard debauchery as a natural human need, to consider violations of morals as the norm.

And the perversions of morality are hidden in that, which low ones do not see; however, God judges them as measures that will decide whether to destroy such a soul as defective or to give it one more chance for correction.

Nevertheless, time is merciless. When it runs out, the norms of evolution will demand Higher beings to accept the decisive, tough measures destroying those who are fallen.

And Higher beings can be understood: If They will not comply with certain evolutionary demands in due time then the door leading Higher up [Above] can be closed for Them as well. Thus, God gives a hard warning to all who are misguided on Earth:

"The time has come to provide answers. I am warning you and instructing you on what should be done to purify the righteous souls

dirtied by their given life and the sins of others. Now I want to prepare these souls for different goals way ahead of time.

He, who is cleansed [purified], will inhibit the physical body again and again, until he achieves a uniform [unified] order in his constructions [structures], and until he comes to understand everything that exists in the Cosmos [Universe].

Those who do not obey will be forgotten, and they will lose their "I."

The visions and signs were given on Earth, but in vain. Humankind did not attempt to compare them with their ugly lives. The by-product of this is the absurdity of actions performed by people.

The twentieth century is the result of Our meticulous work. It highlights a summing up of each one's development. It is the end of the dream of blessing in the Universe and eternal heaven. It is the end of an illusion about the complete forgiveness of sins. It is the end of a lie about the righteousness of sinners and their endless repentance.

The misguided souls will disappear into the void forever. Their punishment will be severe. Thus, I am warning one more time: Do not attempt to get a grip on material wealth in your life. All sins are in it.

Instead, study the Laws of the Universe, Our information; and open your souls to Higher goals.

Man must increase his level of responsibility in everything."

At another time, God speaks about the incorrect behaviour of a human in the following words and addressing every one living on Earth in order for them to understand their lives better.

"Listen and hear your heart! The voice of Reason will send you its messages. Accept them and comprehend them! For there are many souls who lag behind and who heed the voice of low desires, and not the heart.

There is much disobedience. There is much glorifying of thyself.

But only true believers will have My blessings.

Those who have sunk into self-interest [service-to-self] and infamy will be given a harsh penalty. But only after death will the sins be uncovered, as well as an unholy heart sunken in a human's dirt.

Many are proud of their lusts, placing them at the level of an achievement in the name of humanity and showering themselves with undeserved gifts.

Nonetheless, no lusts are needed for Me, but true Faith in a Higher purpose that exists beyond humankind. Wake up your Faith in your heart and carry it day after day, year after year, and century after century. The millenniums will pass, and those still with Me will find blessings and peace in their souls. All they will gather into My dwelling!"

In God's appeals to people, I would like to focus on just one moment, which is precisely at "the end of illusion about an endless forgiveness". New knowledge, revealed to the humankind by Higher beings, now tells us the following: **it is forbidden to sin endlessly and to be forgiven. It is just an illusion,** in which low [inferior] ones hide their weakness of spirit and their inability to let go of their own flaws.

Unending forgiveness destroys the stimulus to fight against one's own sins and the flaws of others. Why fight with them and win if God will forgive them anyway. Thus, instead of getting rid of sin right away, a human repeats it a thousand times. Such delusion prevents him from striving toward perfection and drags him out in time.

The Laws of the Universe, and especially *"The Law of cause and effect,"* affirm something different: Nothing is forgiven for one who has chosen the path of ascending to God.

God can forgive a person only after he has sincerely repented his actions and recognised his sin completely in front of God. Sincere repentance indicates that wrong actions will be prevented from occurring again in the future. Thus, when a human repents, and then sins again, it reveals his hypocrisy and the unawareness of his actions. No forgiving can take place in the absence of sincere repentance. Where there is no awareness, the law of cause and effect is triggered, and the person reaps what he sows.

Indulgence and vice are the Devil's doing only, as they lead the soul to him. The Devil wishes a human to make as many mistakes as possible. The more sins human commits, the more negative energies will be accumulated in his soul; therefore, there will be more chances that this soul will end up with Him. Thus, the Devil wants a person to sin endlessly. Endless sins can only exist on Earth, where the separation of souls takes place. Once a soul ends up with Devil, a harsh education in the negative System begins.

Humans pay for everything through karmic dependency. Even insignificant acts make a difference on a path of ascend: they can elevate the soul, or they can bring it down. A human has to report to his Teacher for each and every step he takes forward or backward.

The Laws of the Cosmos are stern: Whoever has not achieved their developmental goals by a certain time, will be decoded [destroyed] or sent for correction in much more severe conditions in another worlds.

Punishment awaits a human for all the mistakes he made during the course of his life.

This is how the Hierarch speaks of Higher beings who are trying to direct humans onto true path of perfection.

"At the present time, when people are falling far short of the desired result, there is something to think about and to reflect on. But unfortunately, a human does not perceive the information coming to him precisely. Therefore, we repeat the same things all over again. If, once again, nothing has been understood, the situation will be carried over into next incarnation. And, in addition, this unfulfilled program will be added to the human's next life.

Thus, a human is a machine, but with the possibility of choice that We have provided. This small fraction of freedom; however, sometimes drags a person somewhere he should not be; so, he gets

stuck in sins. In this case, he has to either be decoded or to be sent into very low worlds for correction.

By means of work and suffering, the soul can get elevated even higher than on Earth. And this is the only way of salvation that We have invented for those who are misguided. But not everyone can be changed this way, so their souls have to be transformed completely and to be returned to a 'zero' setting, launching a new stage of life and starting everything from the beginning. If the same situation repeats again, then the soul in question has to be decoded again. This is a painful process that represents only a small fraction of what people should know about lost souls for the time being.

The [biological] matter can be remade easily, but souls are very hard to remake; therefore, no one should just completely fall into degradation [retrogression]. Programs such as these have not been given to any soul. In each program there are limitations to degradation, and very often some of the programs end up in death, as a human refuses to understand that he has turned onto the wrong path.

In each program, even for superior individuals, there is a minus effect [negative event], which bestows either blessings as the testing moment, or challenges. It depends on the soul, its comprehension of what is happening, and whether or not it will cope with them.

In the end, everything boils down to one thing: if person wants to slide down – he succumbs to temptations and does not overcome challenges; if he does not want that [refuses temptations] – the minus effect [negative situations] gets minimized with time; is replaced with a positive effect; and sometimes disappears completely. But this can happen only in prominent individuals that are composed solely from positive qualities which they have accumulated during their life. Thus, spirituality and lack of spirituality are two different tendencies in the direction of development and in their essence. However, the person chooses for himself."

Let us take a look at some more contacts from an earlier time.

The text below is spoken by one of the Hierarchs of the "Union."

Naturally, during the contact activity, we were curious about how the soul sees in the subtle world when it has no vision apparatus, or eyes. Thus, one day, we asked a question:

– What can You tell us about the vision of the soul?

The Hierarch responded:

"This topic interests every human, and we can speak a lot about it. Let us say the following.

The vision of the soul is a special kind of vision. The soul sees from all directions at the same time, and this is a volumetric vision. It does not have a special organ of external vision. The subtle shell, which possesses a type of special sensitivity, is involved in this particular process. The shell is made from a special kind of energy conglomerations.

Such conglomerations move very fast, emanating radiance, and transmitting images to the soul. The colour of the soul can even change according to what it sees.

The soul, as a rule, sees differently from the way a physical organ in the material body sees. Your eyes can only see the physical world. And every shell's vision is calculated only for its own world, and not more.

Naturally, only by means of an energy concentration method is it possible to reach this point when the shell starts seeing more subtle worlds as well: one that is near to it in terms of its structure and energy level. For example, physical vision can perceive the astral plane, and the astral plane can see the mental plane, and so on.

The spiritual world is not arranged in the way described to you by the authors of other books. Only the soul can see it after its complete separation from the physical body, when no threads [links] or connections are left. These slow down the ability to reach a spiritual world. Thus, souls that came back, did not reach the spiritual plane. They reached only the astral and mental planes. Besides, there is one more rule in order to get into the spiritual world: an ordinary soul can reach it only through a separator. This is the end of one life and the beginning of the next. Only souls of messengers can escape it [the separator].

Nonetheless, we have gone off subject. Let us return to the vision of the soul. Our Higher [Celestial] world, which serves as a spiritual [world] for humans, is assembled in such a way that it can only be seen by a soul's corresponding subtle body. For example, what you call 'light' is nothing more than the reaction of a vision organ toward special subtle particles.

When the soul transitions from one world into another these colours change. Using your language, it is hard to explain all the complexities of the vision structure in Our World.

If the soul in our world wishes to see something, it sees it, and it surrounds itself with the desired objects. By engaging in what it is wants to do, it progresses [refines]. In other words, this is the soul's world of images. It is located within the Earth plane's boundaries.

By looking at the images which surround the soul, it is possible to determine how far or how little it has progressed in its development. Here also we have our own stairway. The position of soul on these steps is determined according to images created by the soul and the level of sublimity of the images created. This is their world.

By grouping together, the souls create their own cities (to use your language). The inferiors [lower souls] are at the lower steps, and the superiors [higher souls] are at the higher ones. All stairs emanate a special light. The highest ones do not have light; they are lightless. The ones that are slightly lower are white, and those further down are in colour according to your colour spectrum scale.

The colours are emitted by the souls themselves. However, these souls [of colour] desire to rule and to have their subordinates. But this corresponds to their desires, and their level of development.

At each step, the soul's vision becomes more refined, and its range of perception increases. The higher the level on which soul is located the more width it can grasp in one unit of time; thus, the soul's vision improves with its development."

Question: What is the difference between a world where stars are present and one where there are none? Are there some other light sources?

The Hierarch answers:

"The difference is huge. In worlds where are stars, the source of light emanates warmth and energies of a subtle spectrum. The planets that surround the star contribute to the star's work. They send her the energy that supplements its shell. For example, the Earth works for one [one type of] Sun shell, Venus for another, Saturn for a third one, and so on. It is possible for two planets to work for one shell. And all together, the planets provide star light [glow]. An intense exchange [interchange] of energies takes place.

As far as the worlds without stars, the energy there is distributed in a different manner. In such worlds, there are the substitutes of stars, which are entities of a gigantic size that process [convert, transform] the energy which was received from the space-time continuum. They distribute the processed energy to subspaces. In such way, which is stair-like, Cosmos structure forms.

The energy gets transformed at each step [stair, level], and then moves further. This is true of the worlds where there are no stars or planets. The source of light is absent, as the world does not require it. As a rule, light is created for the physical worlds only. In other worlds, the concept of light is created by other means; for example, colour. And the soul can perceive it by means of volumetric vision. The soul, for example, to express it in your language, sees a kind of light, which is actually not a light, but a certain status [condition] of the world. Supposedly, after death, the soul sees not a light at the end of a tunnel, but the world which it is inside, and the world's state and condition."

Question: What can You say about the freedom of the soul?

The Hierarch responds:

"Do you want to ask whether there are free [in leisure] souls? A human understands freedom as complete autonomy and independence. However, any freedom is an illusion. There are no free souls. Everything always belongs to someone; thus, obeys someone. There is always something superior over all. Therefore, freedom in the Universe means belonging to someone; it is like an endless circle.

You can perform something inside the boundaries of this particular circle, but not beyond the allowed margins. Borders are established by the Superiors [Higher beings]. And the soul will stay there [within them] until it reaches next Level. Then, the current borders will be removed, and new ones will be established for it, by the same Higher Level [beings]. Nevertheless, new boundaries will be broader than the previous ones. As an accumulation of spiritual qualities progresses, the boundaries expand further and further. Thus, any freedom has a limit of some kind.

Question: We asked You more than once about the Separator or Distributor; however, we want to clarify this: what happens with the soul of a human who is not subjected to decoding [liquidating]?

The Hierarch answers:

"As stated before, a double review of a human's life takes place in the Separator: a review of situation [of each context] and a review of [each] energy. In the situational review, all life episodes are looked at, including all the details, even small. Then, a life accumulations score is given according to how many different types of energies have been collected. This is done to determine how much energy, given for life, was wasted in vain, and what volume is owed by a human: how much energy he is supposed to bring into the Separator, and how much energy is to be forwarded Above.

The information about his debts, if they are present, is transferred to the programmers and Originators [Institutors]* responsible for that soul, who then decide which situation the human must undergo in the future so he will be able to pay his debts. Thus, there are many complex destinies for many people.

Furthermore, the characteristics of all life's deeds, major and minor, are given. Each main and each minor deed is divided by two categories: good and bad, positive and negative. In conclusion, the amount of positive and negative energy collected [accumulated] during a whole life is counted.

The quality of the soul depends on which kind of qualities it has collected the most.

Since all this cannot occur immediately, the soul stays in the Separator for some time. For Us, it takes just a moment; for you it seems like a few hours, as you and We have a different perception of time.

Nonetheless, We have told you that there are a few Separators, and each race has its own Separator. Therefore, prior to the Separator, the souls undergo an additional dividing by Levels of earth plane. Our machines do this work. In the Separator itself, these Levels are distributed on the staircase accordingly and are grouped, so the process of souls being separated according to their level of development is accomplished quickly and qualitatively.

Sometimes, there are queues to the Separators during the mass soul take away. This is just a small part of what happens to the soul after its death. Thus, a human has to do a lot of thinking."

Question: How does the reconstruction of the Earth take place and by means of which mechanisms?

The Hierarch responds:

"By reconstructing a human, We are reconstructing the energies qualities of the Earth. The main focus is changing people's consciousness. The reconstructing of consciousness influences their lifestyle, their positions in life, their principles, their world view and their moral deeds.

The human starts thinking differently; thus, his actions are in accordance with his standard thinking. In this way, the brain and main working mechanisms of a human are changing as he begins to work with energies of a higher potential.

Nonetheless, by reconstructing a human to the normative indicators needed by Us, We have to, of course, use a very large quantity of energy. However, the energy sent to humans not only reconstructs them, but influences the planet as well.

The energy infiltrates into the Earth's shells where it works like a time bomb. But this is only the beginning. In the end, the Earth and humankind must review their life positions and understand whom they depend on, and where their aspirations should be directed."

Question: What are morals from the energy point of view?

The Hierarch answers:

"The energy of morals is the qualities of the soul, which allows it to exist without any deviations toward the karmic side; consequently, the high energy of morals will not allow the low energy of temptations to take over a human's acts.

The high morals of a human are connected with the accumulations of a high energy range in his matrix.

The matrix accumulations define an individual's Level, forming his morals and dictating his actions.

Each Level of existence operates according to different morals and energy rules. This allows for the soul to see where and to which side its deviations are headed: the karmic side or Divine perfection.

This is like a chain of interdependence: the morals are the rules; and the soul sets up its own rules according to its development Level. The Level of development is a [certain] step of perfection at the energy plane. The energy plane is a stairway toward the Absolute. And the Absolute is an intelligent [thinking] energy, and so on.

Morals are the laws, with the help of which the production of clean energies for the Cosmos is regulated.

The goals for further development are formed with the help of morals. By comprehending [understanding, absorbing] them, the soul can jump up a few steps on the Level plane at once.

If a human does not follow the morals, his soul can get lost in life and in knowledge and will end up not where We are directing it to be. We prefer a straightforward path, without deviations, which only serve to overextend the path to perfection and overspend Our energies.

We gave two paths: one that leads to Devil and one that leads to God. There is no middle [in-between] path. And a human, while learning one or another truth, feels which path is closer to him [inclination]. We offer the ways, but the choice is his."

Question: How much longer will our Solar system exist?

The Chief Determinant of Earth responds:

"The forthcoming century is a century of the golden Sun, as solar radiation on Earth will increase manyfold. However, the Sun's life cycles are reaching the end [completion] of the developmental cycle. The Sun is leaving the horizon of empyrean [ethereal] events; it curtails its program and declines in its life processes. The decrease will be significant, but not immediate.

The program to turn off its life cycles has initiated. The contraction of the star will occur in about two hundred thousand years in the measurement of lifetime.

A black hole will form instead of the compressed Sun, and it will draw all the nearest space inside itself. Nonetheless, it will be a transition into new plane of an existence for all of your Solar system. In conclusion to what has been said: this will be the end of the program of your material system; however, it will transition to a step higher, into a different form of an existence."

Let us now turn toward God's narrations from a later time period, where he expresses his thoughts in a complex language. Through brief messages to humans, He is trying to deliver the light of Divine truths to them and to elevate their Spirits to an appropriate level of understanding.

"As I have spoken, they will possess a positive character in the tactic of preconceptions and assessments about the senseless and invisible, about ethereal and parallel, about constructive and chaotic, expressed dually in the present subjective realistic world outlook.

A great deal is spoken. But only the few will comprehend the truth from what is being said.

Slander [evil speaking] is unacceptable to the writing here. Such substances of Spirit will be destroyed by their own configuration of what they said, as a response and a reverse order; thus, karma.

The Spirit has a potential and is inclined toward the changes. The imperfection of Spirit is comparable only to a figurative stimulation, applied to one part of the Essence*.

The change consists in increasing the potential by means of the accumulation of forms with subjective and consistent constructions that are expressed by one or other constructions of the energy plane.

The comparative feature of realistic expression registers into a single figurative [descriptive] version of Spirit and possesses a sustenance trait [preserves itself].

The subjective reality that is contained in such a manner has the ability to capture a formal partition of the specific concepts from episodic cycles; thus, a selection of qualitative constructive components of Spiritual potential.

The concreteness of volume has the ability to concentrate the qualitative characteristics of comparable energies. This way, the imaginary does not deny the full concept of the natural position of Spirit in matter and in the multileveled physical substances contained in matter.

The substances combine in themselves the qualities of the Unified Spirit that governs all organizational Systems.

In the future, the detailed structure of individual organs in the organism or the organizational system will be shown as separate units or as general detailing, in relation to the Cosmos, inner and outer."

"The time continuum rejects false information, presented in full configuration of one or another kind.

Therefore, it follows that the time continuum governs the masses located below systematic and positive directions, which, in their turn, have a broad spectrum of world views, which gives an opportunity for perfecting in the World System of common conceptions of development, as planetary constructive presentations or as constructions of the lower plane that belong to common comprehensions about the coefficient of Spiritual perfection.

The explanation above compares the facts of common development and the consequences that branch out from the general [common] planning of the world scale development of all regional centres of the universal [ecumenical] type.

The coefficient of world understanding, studied at the present stage of the human development, equals five out of a hundred percent on a standard scale.

This reflects a small part of what a human has from his knowledge about the world structure of the Universe, as well as the adjoining parallel structural beginnings, and also the structural units pertaining to the post-death [after death] plane of physical images.

This small part measures knowledge according to a measurement system of hundred percent (roughly speaking). In reality, knowledge is not measured and is limitless. There is no end to infinity. Anything that begins continues to develop endlessly in two directions: positive and negative. Control over it belongs to Entity who is going through development at the Spiritual plane.

The degradation [retrogression] of the Entity is not a downfall, but a transition onto a different road of development which Entity choses for itself.

Such control over souls is not possible [souls have to pick their own road]. And this is a new fact that We reveal to humans at this particular level of perfecting.

This is the only flaw *(absence of control)** in spiritual development, or to be exact, it is not actually a flaw but rather a control, achieved in this way, over balance of the souls, which are positive and negative. Balance is necessary, so it is kept by this [type of control].

I want to remind you that despite a potential transfer of thought images, it is necessary to foresee the aftermath of one or another thought-containing image, identified by consistent causes of the constructions of the impulse transfer, which belongs to the specifics of actions created by Entities at this given developmental stage.

Watching over the correctness of thought image formation is a control over the information bases that are also regulated by the Entity itself.

The bases are the same for the same Levels. The division of the base, which has a limit to the amount of thought image storage, results in an overbalance. Thus, the division of the base frees it from excess.

The new base received belongs to a construction of the same type as the previous one, and it is calculated strictly for the certain group of thought images created by the Level plane.

The impulse connection gives an opportunity for the progressive development of the configurability of planned constructions, which manifest themselves as specific formations in individual links of the brain apparatus.

The systems of this structure must perform the work of a Higher order, which is about the distribution of thought formatting bases in cosmic space in reference to a pole arrangement in one or another part of space. Such distributions help when space is entered, as the power of thought is key for movement [progression] in it."

"The meaning of what is being said will be revealed to seeking souls. And let their hearts help them with that.

In a state of achieved organism and field structures stimulation, the bio-energy shield strengthens along with an increase to its energy consumption, which is taken from the condition of preservation of the energy complexes. A special place is given to the condition of increased ionization of a whole organism, and especially human cells.

An official manifestation of this comes from the achieved opportunistic time positions that determine the condition of bio-stimulation during an identified time continuum which makes the adaptation of an organism to the Earth's conditions possible and hardens life cycles and the development of potential opportunities in general.

This proves there is a field structure that interconnects with the reality of the certain situations and the integrity of an interaction relative to the whole potential of the egregor [autonomic psychic, spiritual Entity composed of peoples' thoughts which influences the thinking of groups of people].

In a specific example, the received gradation completely adopts human structure and binds it together, without giving in to the deviations of various potential biorhythms.

The wholly built structure of an organism allows a focus on life activity in unity with all the bodies together. Received in such a way the construction will compliment [supplement] Earth and the whole cosmic principle about development as a unified self-developing system which, in turn, is reminiscent of a uniform organ of human indivisibility.

Thus, the conclusions:

1. Indivisibility is a potential sign of integrity, which exists and functions in a unified, indivisible cosmic organism, and so is in any small part or fraction of the same volume.
2. The above is the Law of preservation [retention] and transition. Without indivisibility there is no unity.

In all-embracing provision of existing connection [link] there is something looking like a whole [holistic] organism that develops according to an identical law of the contained inside it a smaller organism, and the same is true of inner and outer space, and so on.

Laws are the same for everyone."

"In a broad spectrum of world foundations [frameworks] of new tendencies, an understanding of the Absolute* as the unifying and sole beginning of everything that exists, has prevailed. However, that is not quite right.

The beginning of everything that exists took its first breath thanks to the unity of all in its Essence in a single time segment figuration plus [together with] a given norm of substance at the definite quantitative proportion related to an atomic structure, produced by a special energy potential system of cardinal relationships that belong to spiritual world.

The bond between atom and molecule may be described as the relationship of one single holistic unit to another one of the same nature, but they have relatively different systems of graphic image construction and spatiotemporal [space-time] connections.

This necessitates making a touchpoint with the utmost tangents of the given worlds in a light form of identical contacting link.

As such, the interchange between the energy field's structural units and stimulation through given transition in the touchpoint of a single contact field communication between two worlds takes place.

This small detail has great significance for providing answers to many of your questions about the formation and transition from one world into another that are linked with each other by the definite relativity and duality of meanings in units of volumes, which are received by touching [connecting] with one another.

Accordingly, [We] are speaking of unity and uniting.

The worlds are in relative order between the components of one whole; however, each of them has the same whole as well.

I am talking about forthcoming events.

I am talking about existence and transformation received after transition.

I am talking about the human facets in the world and the world's [facets] in the space.

What shall be spoken perfectly – shall be rendered in a perfect image.

Comprehended in this way, reality has a dual meaning. It is life and transition; thus, it is the replacement of shells for more perfect ones."

God's appeal to representatives of the sixth race:

"My worlds of impulse modification will be addressed to an Upper class of the sixth race; Upper class – in a spiritual understanding of self-developing.

There is a time and place that are prepared for your souls in order to ascend faster in the spiritual and material plane at the same time. Precisely by combining one with the other, the newest modification of the unified holistic construction will be achieved.

Your goal is to regenerate and to develop the initiative achievement network of the Spirit in matter [the body]. This will be much in many.

The particles of My Higher principle will interpret Faith, Knowledge and the urge for a single [unified] Goal on which the mass ascent of Hierarchy's steps is established.

Mass character expressed in a simultaneous action by many of ascending in one step their progression in the spiritual plane, as well as in the material one. Any incompetency in this matter should be transformed into a desire to see and to learn.

Great desire gives birth to a tendency for perfection factors to accelerate, showing superpowers and higher standards in external events which are suppressed in a human organism at the present time.

As a whole, the advent of the sixth race of humankind presents a precondition for the total development of a Godlike human state, the final result of which will be presented after the completion of the seventh race – the final stage in human perfection.

Further on, a significant impulse for understanding cause-and-effect system-code actions will take place, and the transformations and

transitions from the space of one world into the space of another [world] will be completed; and so on, into infinity.

The meaning of the human code will exhaust itself in the rhetoric of understanding of it, as the brain apparatus [of a human] is not calculated for an infinite acceptance of the information of cosmic education; and, in its finite objectivity, it delays the development of the spiritual plane.

Big tasks face highly potential individuals of the sixth race; and invariably a maximum effort is required of them, so our common goals can be achieved."

I will leave these texts without comments. Let everyone who reads understand them according to their level of comprehension of new knowledge.

CHAPTER 5

THE ACCELERATION OF HUMAN SPIRITUAL DEVELOPMENT

One man asked us: "Why has God entrusted His Laws to you, and not to me? What is the difference between me and you?"

To that, I responded to: "You only think about yourself, and we think about others. This is the difference."

While reflecting on questions about human development and imagining an unending staircase of souls ascending toward God, I saw, regretfully, how much longer a human must still go in his comprehension in order to reach the top of God's Hierarchy. It is billions and billions of years in our [Earth] time: so long that is hard for a human to imagine.

Furthermore, even while on the Earth plane, he must scale hundreds of Levels of development, and this takes thousands of years; the countless amounts of incarnations and reincarnations, and the tiresome glimpses of short lives, in comparison with eternity.

But when will a human become worthy for even the first Level of Divine Hierarchy, in which eternity will open up for him and he will stop dying and being resurrected thousands of times? And I mused on how to accelerate the ascent of human souls and to minimize their sufferings on Earth.

It is possible, of course, to use the way of Devil by making rigid programs without a freedom of choice, as the development's slowdown occurs exactly because that freedom of choice was permitted. A human is endlessly confused by what is needed and what he wants; and he is endlessly straying from where he needs to be; thus, he is being returned at some initial point, by means of the reincarnation and karma systems.

A soul that ends up with Devil, reaches all the qualities that He decides are necessary for it. Whether an individual wants it or not, he fulfils exactly what is written in his program and what the Devil orders him to do.

The selection [accumulation] of qualities happens in this way: an analysis is made of which qualities are already there, and which ones need to be collected in order for the soul to reach the next step. Then, the situations, which, by being worked through, will contribute to accumulation of the needed energy types, are developed. The individual cannot avoid difficult situations. God, on the contrary, grants his soul this opportunity.

Nonetheless, God could have adopted the Devil's system of accelerated development. However, he has rejected it for some reasons, as he considers it unacceptable for him. Based on that, I decided to ask Him:

– Why don't You remove the freedom of choice from a soul's development in order to accelerate its progress in same way as the negative Hierarch [Devil] did?

– A freedom of choice is the main thing that differentiates My system of soul development from negative Hierarchy's. I need conscious creators and loving followers. I will not speak much. You know precisely what freedom of choice gives. It serves as a separator of souls at the Earth plane. By making a choice, the soul, as a result, ends up either with Me or with the Devil.

– Are there any other ways to speed up a human's development? – I asked. – These endless reincarnations take so much time! Thus, many people would agree to accelerate their development and would even undertake rigid programs.

– This is good question. However, I have a question which you, yourself, must try to answer. What comments do you have in regard to improving of Our work on Earth? Can you provide Us with some suggestions for an improvement of work among the people? We see your life from Above, from our Higher positions, and you see it from Below. You are at the midst of life, and you have a personal view about it. We would like to know your point of view. Let it be your next exam.

And we began thinking over the question, not about how to improve a human's life of, but about how to accelerate his development, so he could transition to God's Hierarchy sooner and became worthy of its first level.

God does not have any interest in a human's material wealth and his [human's] life in tranquillity and happiness. This is what actually corrupts the soul and constantly slows down its progression for hundreds and thousands of years. But a human does not want to understand this. In his head, there is a lasting illusion that God is trying to make people happy and to create a haven on Earth for that purpose, so they can lounge, lecher, and regress; a human, by having low level of consciousness, is unable to make himself work for the greater good and to perfect his soul. He only does so when there is a threat to his prosperous existence or for the sake of some perspective of a better life.

When such a person's material level increases, he plunges into the pleasures momentarily by eating a lot, drinking, watching spectacles, travelling, and wasting his free time on empty pastimes.

God does not need human bodies, He needs perfect human souls; therefore, He will not allow them to regress due to an excess of wealth. An individual gets showered with excessive goods by the Hierarch of the negative System in order to confuse his soul and to lead it toward regression, so it can belong to Him in the end. Only a few are able to manage their wealth correctly, using it to perfect the soul and not for pleasure.

Nevertheless, any detail offers a hint [fine detail]. There is always some kind of a margin, which, once it has transitioned over to one or another side [positive or negative], starts to delay development [evolution]. A low-level soul is perfected in poverty. However, the median or high-level soul, when placed in poverty, will delay its perfection, as the progression of different Levels requires the investment of certain funds.

For example, in order for a human to develop [evolve] intellectually, he has to be taught to think in a chosen direction at university. An aircraft designer has to be taught to master numerical operations, to draw, and to have a special type of thinking. And when he creates a new plane project, funds are then needed to put this model to use.

In order to teach, educational establishments must be built, teaching personnel trained, projects created, manufactured and implemented into life. And it requires large resources for a layer of intellectuals at a certain Earth Level to be able to exist and develop there. And the higher a soul climbs up on the steps of the evolution, the more resources it requires. Thus, there is a natural correspondence between Level of development and the extent of provision it requires. The same goods that support development on one Level, will serve to delay it on another level, becoming excessive.

Thus, two extremes interfere with soul's progress in positive direction: an excess of resources and their limitation, which, of course, are decided for each soul individually.

Nevertheless, we were given a specific task: to reveal the finer details about existence and say at what expense it would be possible to accelerate a human's progression. Therefore, I began to analyse modern life not from a human point of view, but from the perspective of new knowledge received from Higher beings.

I have included suggestions on how to correct things in the life of a modern society that I did not like and saw as curbing the soul's perfection.

Once I had prepared a list of suggestions, I encouraged my husband, Aleksandr Ivanovich, to read it; and he also made his additions. And at the regular contact [planned communication session], we began speaking about the acceleration of human development on the Earth plane.

– At the last contact we spoke about the acceleration of humankind's progression, – I began. – We have not invented anything new; however, some isolated points can be used for the correction of a human's life organizational methods and his upbringing. Let us read this to You now.

– Of course, please. – X*… (God's cosmic name) agreed.

– We offer to improve the structure of a human who has a high developmental Level. The spiritual individual, for example, at the expense of implementing new functions in his bio-matter [physical body], should eat once a day. There is too much time lost on the consumption of food. Firstly, money must be earned for this food, and then the produce must be bought and prepared. Some women are always busy with just the food preparation, such as breakfasts, lunches, and dinners. All day is spent just for this. A woman who is underdeveloped [unskilled] can find the satisfaction in it and acquire some practical skills; however, for a woman of median [medium] Level this is unacceptable, as the soul yearns to be busy with some intellectual work or creativity, but because of the existing organization of family relationships, she cannot do it. Thus, that woman sacrifices her own progression for the sake of a duty to her family. Also, it would be helpful to shorten night rest time for individuals who are involved with intellectual and creative work. They want to achieve a lot during the day, but the need for sleep obstructs their plans.

– Sleep can be reduced to three or four hours a day, but it should not damage the health, – my husband added.

– And all these reductions are necessary, so there will be more time left for creative and intellectual work, – I emphasized.

– Such changes in a man's behaviour will demand, first of all, a correction in many structures of a human body, – confirmed X*…– In order for a human to eat once a day and to sleep four hours and be sufficient, many processes have to change, and the functioning of the subtle shells have to become more complex. However, everything is possible. We have a similar single case in practice.

– It would be nice to correct the construction itself in highly evolved individuals, as it is often the case that a human wants to progress, but his physical capabilities will not let him, – reaffirmed Alexandr Ivanovich.

– I understand, – responded X*…

– It is possible to create a link between a human's life span and his progression, so as to make such connection in his program, – I offered and explained: – There are people who live long, and, in our opinion, absolutely purposelessly. Such people can be removed. And those who are progressing…

– What do you mean by remove? Completely? Decode? – clarified X*…, without letting me finish talking.

– No, not to decode, but just stop a program and replace it with new one, which will allow further progress.

– So, you are saying that their program must be improved? – X*… asked again.

– Correct, – I confirmed. – Because we see many old people who live long, up to eighty or ninety years; nevertheless, their life is absolutely empty. It is not filled with anything. Nonetheless, we remember, as it was mentioned at one of the contacts that the soul perfects through the sufferings. However, what we do see is that many elderly people live in contentment, and they just enjoy their idleness. Such a soul is not progressing. It does not wish for anything, does not learn anything, and just enjoys resting. However, there are also elderly people who work intellectually and have creative hobbies. We understand that even writing memoirs is a creation and intellectual work that analyses a life lived. These memoirs are not needed by people, but by the soul itself. The soul continues its perfection through them. And when such an old person dies without finishing his work, we feel that this is unfair. It makes sense to design [program] in such way that life extends for those who are progressing and shortens for those who put stop to their development. Let long life to be a compliment for the person for his aspirations and the unstopping work of his soul.

– Right, – He responded uncertainly.

– And on the contrary, there are cases when life ends prematurely for a creative person. He dies young. In our opinion, this is not quite right. An opportunity should be given to him to develop in his direction until the maximum level of professionalism possible, – added Alexandr Ivanovich.

– There is more with regard to short lives, – I pinned down. – Some people live eleven or twenty years and die. We already know that this could be connected with a human's energies debts; however, is such a short life justified economically? Such large expenses were used for the birth of a human, along with a not very effective childhood and an adolescence and abrupt death thereafter.

I have always reacted oversensitively toward premature life departures, even of people that were absolutely unknown to me; but it has also happened to me to see the deaths of familiar people and young people. My soul, like the soul of every normal individual, has protested against it. However, despite knowing the cosmic reason for early deaths (short lives are given specially in order to repay past energy debts), I decided to seek a way for extending their further existence once their debts are paid. Thus, I did my presentation from the perspective of economy.

– We suggest switching people to a different development program once they have paid off their debt in the requested quality. As such, the economy of energies spent on birth and a child's body development will be achieved, at last. The economy can be achieved in adolescence as the human already received some kind of education which can be used for resolving new tasks. You can then decide into which program he can be transferred.

– Well, this is good, – X*... agreed.

– We feel that such a program will be more economical, – I carried on. – And one more thing: can we extend the efficiency of the Determinant while he is leading a human, meaning giving him more opportunities to motivate his pupil toward the goal and to be able to implement changes in his program in order to accelerate his perfection? Determinants should be allowed to manipulate a human more in life situations. It happens often...

– Stop there, – God held me back. – You suggest that Determinant acts on his own initiative?

– Yes, on his own, as it happens that the person who wants to do something useful, cannot do so because of insufficient education and experience that make him unable to determine what would be the best for him. Thus, at this moment, the Determinant could give him a nudge in the right direction, right away.

– I think that this is excessive, – objected X*...– A human must seek and find on his own.

– We also think that it is necessary to increase the amount of activity options for creative individuals.

– On Earth?

– Yes, at least on Earth, for right now, and after, in the Hierarchy as well.

– Are there not enough fields of work for people?

– Yes, because the choice of activity is always limited. Sometimes, a person would like to do something new besides what he already has mastered; however, he feels that for some reason he cannot. Obviously, this is because it was not implemented into his program. This way, it will be possible for average and above average [higher developed] souls to find out something else in addition.

– Do you think that a human must be occupied by some other creative activity?

– I do. The program should have more options to choose from. For example, there is a wonderful tendency that has been implemented already, wherein one creative individual masters a few types of creative activities. In our view, this is great. But more people should be involved in it.

– Yes, sure, – He agreed.

– It is possible to expand it, – I continued. – Next. We feel that a freedom of choice in the situations can be reduced from thirty percent [currently] to ten for low [developed] individuals. They could be in more rigid situations: it will discipline them better. As we are observing at the present time, low individuals use the freedom given them for a complete degradation. Thus, whenever they face rigid conditions, they develop well and accumulate some positive qualities.

This suggestion, made by me, was based on some observations.

One young man known to me, has done well while in army. He wrote beautiful, kind letters to his mother. Once he returned from army, he tasted a life of leisure, booze and sprees; and the conscientiousness that he once had, left him without a trace.

He grew stupid and hard-hearted. His rapid degradation began. He ended up in prison. When he faced harsh conditions there, he started reflecting on his life once again, repented, and glimpses of intellect began showing up in his letters to his mother. Then, there was an amnesty, and he was let out before serving his full sentence. And once again, everything has repeated itself. He was unable to use his freedom for the soul's progression.

Another young man, who has been in prison more than once, admitted to his mother that when he was free he did not know how to live and what to do to keep himself busy; but in the prison, there is order, in his view, and he felt he was being led in the right direction. Life there is strictly planned and determined ahead of time.

Naturally, those are very young evolutionary souls, and they demand lots of attention for themselves from society. The society must direct them, discipline them, occupy them with creativity, sports, and with some useful labour. Absence of work leads them to the negative System.

X*... clarified my suggestion:

– Do you suggest limiting their freedom of choice, that is, reducing the amount of choices in their program?

– I do, – I reaffirmed.

– Understood. Please continue.

– With significant deviation from a human's preassigned program of tasks, if no correction is possible, it [the program] should be stopped, so that an individual does not have time to deteriorate too much. It makes more sense to prevent regression than to decode the souls or to forward them to the negative System. Thus, one more suggestion: time freed from household chores can be used for a human's creative activities; thus, the soul can accumulate positive energies. Some people have very little free time for a spiritual development, so time used for domestic chores can be released for that. For example, women spend lots of time taking care of their family.

– We already resolved this issue, and in some countries, household appliances have freed woman from excessive household duties. Here [in the former Soviet Union], this issue has not yet been resolved. However, with time, it will be same way as in America. Ready-to-cook meals will be stocked in stores, and everything will be fine.

– Oh, and we wanted to suggest the following as well: to use more semi-finished [ready-to-cook] products.

– It will be that way, no worries.

– In everyday life, it would be nice to improve processes, instead of washing dishes, for example, to use disposable ones; and for housewives not to do laundry [by hand]. Instead, this time can be used for a creative work.

– Do you mean to replace individual labour by machines?

– Yes, of course. But from another point of view, we have noticed that machines demand a lot of time for servicing.

– Ok, this is how we understood you: non-spiritual people should not have the supporting equipment, as it is better for them to do everything by themselves for educational purposes.

– But of course, – I confirmed. – This helps them to accumulate work skills and a sense of a duty toward their family. When busy with household duties, there is no free time left to be used for degradation. But those, who have aspirations for spiritual development, should have more machinery, so they can have free time for their development. Thus, household work shortens, and free time increases for development.

– What you are referring to implies better financial provision for the spiritual category of people, – remarked X*…

– Definitely, – I agreed. – Those who wish to perfect the soul, require conditions to be made for the realization of their aspirations. Some people, for example, want to study, but they do not have the resources. When progressive desires surface, the resources should be available for their accomplishment. If this were the case, the Determinant should be given more freedom.

– Understood. Go ahead.

– In general, heavy physical labour dulls a human significantly, and all thoughts go away from his head. We have experienced this ourselves.

– Yes, that is correct.

– Thereby, as was done before, society could possibly be divided into categories [tiers], but with amendments made for modern time and the current developmental level. Those who are unable to think, could be involved in a physical labour, and those who are in the middle could do creative, organizational and administrative work, trying to master a higher mental [intellectual] activity. Now, for example, many intellectuals have no choice but to be forced into physical labour and into activities that are not fit for them. I understand, of course, that this is due to the transitional period; however, it should be reconsidered in the future. In other words, the activities should be divided according to Level.

– And should they be compensated according to that?

– Yes. However, all this should be decided by the Determinants and Originators [Developers] in the Higher Spheres. They know which soul belongs to which developmental Level and what should be predetermined for it. If we leave this decision to the people, then the lowest ones would be highly paid, and the high [highest] would get paid the least, as people do not appreciate the same qualities as You do. The people are not yet able to determine Levels of their development appropriately.

– Do you feel that a highly spiritual individual has to be financially secure?

– Yes. This, in our opinion, should stimulate development. He [spiritual individual] should not sacrifice himself in the name of his family, working day and night to support them financially. A highly spiritual human must earn enough by working eight hours to support his family and to have time to perfect his soul in the desired direction. Or, another scenario might be considered, such as to have servants in the households of highly spiritual individuals.

– But there is a hidden danger: a highly spiritual individual can fall into regression. Lots of money and lots of free time could corrupt the soul. A human will not direct his efforts toward the right path. Thus, for some humans, conditions such as having little money and no servants can protect them from deterioration. The human is then completely busy, and he has no time for degradation. What we are striving to achieve is for humans to be fully occupied.

– But it is necessary to manoeuvre during their upbringing. Thereby, we suggest such scenarios where the Determinant can, depending on situation, promptly govern an individual. What is good for one [person], is not good for another. If the Determinant can regulate situations more, then, in the right moment, when human just starts deteriorating, He can decrease his freedom and his financial well-being, and thus prevent his further decline by doing this. Sometimes, it is important not to tempt humans with something, but to turn them away from temptations, especially when many are asking [to be turned away]. Thus, it is important not to allow a human to sin.

– Understood. Go on.

– The implementation of servants in well-off families who practice spiritual development would help, firstly, to free time for creative and intellectual activities in creative individuals; and, secondly, society would be more occupied; and thirdly, it would discipline less developed Levels and would create an example of aspiration for them.

– All right. Go ahead.

– Regarding household appliances. We have to think about improving them. But despite freeing lots of time, they require lots of time for servicing as well.

– That is unclear. Please explain. Why do they require lots of time to be serviced?

– They have to be washed, cleaned, repaired, loaded and unloaded.

– This is because your technology is bad. Robotic machines exist – you just do not know about them yet. But they already exist. These machines are completely automated and will eliminate many intermediate functions.

– Pardon us; it looks like we are lagging behind.

– Do you have anything else?

– You have said already that in the future sixth race childhood and old age will be organized differently; however, it could take at least another five hundred years before the new human structure can start performing; and until then, the old human model will be used; thus, there is time left for better use of old age and childhood for the soul's perfection. There should be more opportunities for creativity, ideas, and arts and crafts.

– In your opinion, whenever there is a freedom – then there is idleness?

– Yes.

– I see.

– And it would be nice to occupy children more with creativity, sport, and some useful activity.

– Understood.

– Lower souls also strive to create; thus, creativity can be divided into a more primitive type for young souls and a more refined one for higher souls. However, we must try involving everyone in creativity from a young age.

– Do you suggest making creativity multileveled?

– Yes. It would help upbringing. It would even be possible to use creativity in this way starting not at low human developmental Levels, but at the animal Levels. As animal souls transition into a human form, we observe that upbringing starts at their developmental stage already. Some animals can be trained very easy, and they are able to accumulate creative skills too. They can act on stage and master movements which are not inherent to their animal world. Thus, at the given developmental stage of a soul's development, it would be possible to further teach them primitive skills.

– All right.

– Also, I want to talk more precisely about a woman's structure. It is not comfortable enough: the processes related to childbearing are very unpleasant for developed souls. They are degrading. It would be good to make some improvements in that direction. We consider childbearing to be a very inferior process. Thus, for higher souls we would like to suggest the creation of children in test-tubes. Children can be grown in labs and their growth observed. This would also free up a woman's time; and, from another point of view, people would be able to regulate the formation of a child's physical body better.

– Good. Anything else?

– All who desire to learn should be given an opportunity.

– And who is not? – He chuckled.

– Those who do not desire are better to be involved with primitive work, – Aleksandr Ivanovich entered the conversation. – They can be simply involved with physical labour if they like it better.

– All right. I understand. But at some point, either at old age or after five reincarnations, he [a human] will have a desire to learn.

– As soon as such a desire appears in him, he should be given an opportunity to study, – I added.

– Good. This question also has a connection with financial well-being. In relation to that, I want to say the following. When a human is given money, it is necessary to foresee possible consequences. You must see the future of a human and how money can influence him, and in which way it can change his behaviour. There is no sense in giving money to lazy people, as it will increase their inaction, and spirituality will not even cross their minds. Human karma needs to be taken into account, making sure that the money will not interfere with it. Even if you start having money and wish to share it with your close ones, you will have to make sure that it will not cause damage to their perfection; otherwise, you could create karma for yourself due to inappropriate kindness and inappropriate distribution of funds. For the future, take this into consideration. And now you can continue.

– There is one more suggestion, human memory should be improved: bad memory delays mastering new knowledge, and also slows down general development. However, more consideration of this is necessary because, at the same time, a good memory can develop parasitism in a human.

– Do you think that a highly spiritual individual has to have a good memory?

– Yes. Nevertheless, the Determinant has to manoeuvre in order to lead a human correctly: in some cases, his memory should be good, and in others it should be bad; thus, controlling the formation of qualities in a human.

– Anything else?

– Also, we are quite worried about the human disbelief in Your existence. We have spoken to humans so many times, and they still do not believe, really.

– There are many disbelievers, of course, but there are also many of those who believe. Everyone believes in his own way.

– Until a human sees the miracle he will not believe completely, – concluded Aleksandr Ivanovich. – Wouldn't it make sense to openly show him a "flying saucer" [UFO] as a miracle, or aliens who have a physical body? They fly to Earth any way.

– People will not see this phenomenon as a miracle as they do not connect it with Me, God. "Flying saucers," in their minds, are connected with the activities of higher civilizations that exist on different planets.

– But it could be a stimulus for development, – insisted Aleksandr Ivanovich.

– There are humans who have seen this and concealed it, because of personal reasons. It has already happened, and it is not new. Such spectacles do not produce much result; nonetheless, they do show the abilities of an Intellect. However, on Earth, there is enough information about it. And if somebody showed an interest toward "flying saucers," he could then seek out information about them, and it would be enough for him. He would not need any miracles anymore, – explained X*…

– But in order to boost human consciousness they [people] need to meet with something unusual, – I supported my husband. – Maybe for the future, a holographic miracle can be invented, so it could then be repeated in the same way two hundred years from now; so, basically, invent and send miracle in a form of a hologram, and repeat after two hundred years. Such omens could push human consciousness into thinking about Higher beings and other planes of existence.

– Or it might be not the omen; but another scenario, making close, material contact with extra-terrestrials [aliens], – Aleksandr Ivanovich developed his idea further, – in order for a human not to regard himself as a tsar of nature, but to acknowledge that he is way behind, compared to many, and that there is a someone else who can really govern the world.

– Do you want the aliens to bring knowledge about Me to the people?

– Yes. Let a human know that others in the Cosmos [Universe] know and respect You. Also, a human must see his inferiority, as everyone has such big opinion about himself.

– So as to acknowledge the low level of the development… – repeated X*…reflectively.

– Certainly, – I reassured. – It will be a boost and a stimulus for further development.

– All right, maybe We will do so, but in a different way: by showing the difference between humans and Higher beings.

– We see from the Beneath that such an effective boost is needed, – I repeated. – All people's thoughts are currently directed toward receiving a maximum amount of pleasure. And this will show them all the pettiness and uselessness of their aspirations. The soul must strive toward getting to know the other worlds, other forms of lives, and not smouldering after a mug of a beer or wine. A human must see the emptiness of his actions.

– Good. Understandable. Do you have any more suggestions?

As I had spoken with pathos, He sensed that we are at the end of the conversation. I reaffirmed:

– This is all for right now. But this is not everything yet. I have to think more.

– You have wonderful suggestions. This is not an earthly comprehension of a human behaviour already. You sorted out most things correctly. A human bases his suggestions with regard to how he can live better in material wellbeing and happiness, but yours were based on how the soul can progress further. That is very important. Thank you.

The following week after this contact, Aleksandr Ivanovich had a dream right before awakening, probably in order to recall something. In the dream, we were sitting university entry exams and we had received two fives [the highest grades in the former Soviet Union]. When he told us about it in the morning, the thought came into the head of our daughter Larissa that the Determinant was showing us the grade we had been given in our cosmic exam.

We were very glad to receive such grades; however, we were very aware that we had said very little on a subject that we could have developed more. Nonetheless, we did not expect such a high score. We felt happiness in our souls from the fact that we had accomplished something, meaning that we were moving forward. One must learn to think based not on material wealth, which everyone now began to be obsessed with, but on the benefits for the soul.

CHAPTER 6

DEGRADATION FROM ASSOCIATION WITH LOWER LEVELS

God speaks:

"This talk is about the premature and intercontinental plane, which puts the brakes onto the ascending system of civilized hierarchies of Higher status [rank].

A constant dependence of Levels of Higher orders on lower planes is expressed in this, wherein the constructive possibility of Higher planes is destroyed by the actions influenced by lower Levels who penetrate and force their ideas onto the structure of higher located planes.

Those who are susceptible are subjected to a dependence of such formed relationships, which leads to the subsequent submissive order of the impending lower planes.

The Hierarchy does not allow penetrations into the essential shells of such Levels. Thus, the question in only about the length of time of such penetrations that leave from the Hierarchical stairway of essential inheres.

As the result, such dependency will not be defeated, as the Earth became used to having low grade continuum, which will lead to further degradation of the essence of the Earth.

I will allow it, and, most likely, the decoding of the planet is inevitable; however, not of its whole essential structure, but the partial one. Low episodes of life situations that lead to degradation will be deleted.

The memory of Earth will undergo transcoding [recoding] at this given plane of existence. Its further development will depend on itself [the Earth] and on the work of the Determinant of its Entity, which will be leading it to the next stage of development.

However, the capitulation of coding formations will be possible only in its final developmental stage, meaning that the program can be disabled only in the end-of-life scenarios.

A new form of progression will constructively change the dependable condition in the Hierarchical system of distribution from lower planes, which, in turn, will not be able to influence people because the Earth will not allow them near humans. A new reconstructed form will help Her in this.

To penetrate into human objects will be possible only if the people themselves wish it so. Those people at this current stage, have no consciousness of the actions of such a plane and their dependency on it.

Nonetheless, the simultaneous rise of the individual's level of consciousness will help to overcome low grade actions and to choose the ones that are worthy of the Highest."

Let us try to understand the details of what is being said.

Each higher located Level is influenced by a lower plane. This is how the structure of the connections between the worlds and systems of Hierarchy works.

And even though Higher [Highest] ones have always belonged to the governing Systems and program all that belongs to a lower plane, they are not completely independent from them. There is an energy interdependence between all Levels. The worlds are constructed in such way that Higher beings have use of what is produced for them by a lower layer.

If we take, for example, any middle Level, it turns out that it produces [generates] the energy for a higher-ranking Level and consumes the energy of a lower plane. And it is the same for the first Level to the last in the hierarchical pyramid.

Nevertheless, whilst ascending toward the last plane, the importance of the first [plane] diminishes; however, it does not disappear completely.

Let us take a look at the Earth plane and the first Level of Hierarchy, as they are adjacent [neighbouring] and understood most.

This is the work scheme for two adjacent planes, Higher and lower. According to its needs and Superior main goals, the Higher plane plans and programs the work of the lower plane.

Some separate programs descend into the lower plane through souls that are sent out into the given world.

The souls are mechanisms of the lower worlds' transformation and energy generators for the Highers' needs. From this dual work, the souls also receive payment in the form of energy, which accumulates in the matrix and provides for their growth. Participation in this scheme, therefore, allows a soul to build up its might and potential.

Based on the programs, linked to each incarnated soul, the world is transforming on the inside. Nonetheless, it also has its own program of development, which is global; and all individual mini programs are connected to it and adjusted to its goal. This is a complex interconnection of the programs. However, the program of the world is more stable in comparison with the individual programs, and it is prepared for longer terms. Mini programs are short lived, and it is very convenient to make the correction of the overall program of the Level at their expense.

After the incarnation of souls with their programs, in order for them to begin producing energies for the Superiors, they are sent energy of a certain quality which engages the souls into working according to their programs. The souls start engaging the additional energies from the surrounding environment into the work. Their complex transformation throughout the technological processes, designed for this given world, takes place.

The new types of energies produced are taken above by the Superior Level. This level takes part of these energies for itself, and another part is sent higher Above after a special processing that raises its order [Level, vibrations]. Lower quality energies of are sent Below, and by transforming them, a higher spectrum [of energies] is produced.

Lower Level would not be able to work if the energy were not sent to it from Above. However, the higher Level would also not be able to develop if the lower world did not deliver energies to them. There always has to be more energy produced than the energy sent out or used, so there is always more energy going up than coming down. This concludes an extended production.

A similar system of interdependence proves that the higher Level cannot exist without the lower, as it is based on it, which makes it dependant on the lower plane.

The interdependent influence of one on another is very strong. If the higher Level makes a mistake in its reckonings of something, the lower world will not function, and this will lead toward the degradation not only of the lower plane but of the higher one too.

We are interested in the Earth plane specifically, so we will deal with it in more detail. The earthly world appears as Superior for the certain plane that is located in a parallel existence in relation to a physical world. The lower world, with which humankind is interconnected, and where low [inferior] energies that nourish this world are discarded by humans, is located on the inside of Earth.

That is to say, that by passing the energies through his shells and through the layers-filters of Earth, a human sends high spectrum energies into the Superior plane, and a coarse, low spectrum gets discarded to Earth, to its special System in particular that transforms them.

In the lower world, there is not just one form of existence, but a few, just like in our world. Some entities from the lower world are able to infiltrate our world and influence people with low potential, in other words, those with young souls. There are many individuals among these people who succumb to the influence of the lower plane and commit actions that lead their souls toward degradation.

Being in parallel existence and invisible to humans, these low entities are able to penetrate his subtle constructions and to influence his behaviour and development. They feed on human energy; thus, they are very interested in contacting him. They are energy parasites alike.

They have a high energy potential, and by using it for their self-interest, they bend the aforesaid people to their will and command them. This is expressed as possessions of a different kind.

In young, low-developed souls, as their individual potential is less it cannot protect them.

According to the law of the universe, a high potential subdues a low, so these entities impose various negative actions onto an individual.

They cannot change an individual's program or assign him a new one; they may, however, exploit situations in an individual's program skilfully. For example, when an individual passes through a situation that is in his program, they always direct his actions toward low deeds. That is to say, they skilfully direct by hypnosis an individual's choice to fit their own interests.

By committing low deeds, a human produces negative energies, which nourish low entities which build up their potential and might. And the human degrades [regresses], as he makes choices toward low [bad] and not high [good].

The entities, who penetrate humans' subtle shells, get so used to humans that some of them even master verbal speech, and, through the speech apparatus of a human, can express their low thoughts. When they speak through human, he talks non-sense or yells some entreaties. The ecclesiastics name these entities petty [trivial] demons. But they are energy parasites. There are many parasites on the earth plane, including energy ones.

A human can fight them off. It will be sufficient to exercise one's will power and not succumb to the provocation; not swear and keep one's thoughts pure. Low actions and thoughts nourish these low entities and help them penetrate a human construction.

If an individual is unable to fight them off, another human with higher potential can help him by means of reciting prayers. Thus, a high energy projectile is developed, and it electrocutes them. They cannot take this attack, and they leave the human shell.

Obviously, such entities work for the Devil's negative System, without realising it. By provoking a person into committing low [inferior] deeds, they can lead a weak-willed individual into a total regression. Accordingly, said soul will either be decoded or passed on to Devil. Therefore, a human should learn to resist any low ideas and thoughts that suddenly crop up in his mind. They might not belong to him but to some entities, and often it is so.

Their direct influence by means of contacting an individual's shell affects only certain layers; and they [low entities] function only until the fiftieth Level of Earth's Hierarchy. In this case, we mean that these entities cannot get through the boundaries of Earth's plane. Their influence does not spread because of the prevalence of high consciousness and the energy potential of individuals who do not obey them. Nevertheless, an indirect influence on higher [superior] Levels persists.

Such entities are not able to go higher than the Earth's plane because of the special protective mechanisms that have been created in its constructions.

The Laws of Hierarchy do not allow a forceful influence on someone's will. Even the Teachers of humankind do not have right to supress their pupils' free Will, as this is a human's path of development.

Low entities, as offenders, violate the laws for their selfish goals. However, as they cannot violate the common laws of development completely, they are compelled to do it only temporarily. Any trespassing is temporary. Nevertheless, through the influence of some entities on others, it is possible to detect an individual's shortcomings and weak spots. However, there are many young souls involved in sports or who have some favourite hobbies; thus, due to their positive aspirations they are able to resist the provocation of low entities.

The reason for the emergence of such parasitic forms lies in the Earth itself, as she was being used by low individuals for their personal gain. Thus, the planet, as a huge live soul that has freedom of choice, must refuse having these entities, choosing for herself positive technology of several processes.

Higher beings are not happy with the Earth's "behaviour" and her many processes. Thus, they hold a resentment not just toward the humankind but toward the planet herself. In particular, humans' excessive interest in material goods, in their opinion, comes from the Earth that sort of hypnotises a human and imposes material aspirations on him instead of spiritual ones.

By aspiring for them [material goods], a human lowers his Level and thus produces low energies that is of interest to the Earth. Instead of returning maximum energies to Higher beings, a human gives most of them to the lower plane; thus, producing waste from a Cosmic point of view.

Consequently, the Celestial Teachers posed a serious question not just to humanity but to the Earth that the time had now come to rethink and turn toward spiritual development.

The Earth is a vast soul; nevertheless, it can miscalculate and make mistakes. It also slows down humankind's development, as they are interconnected. Naturally, such big souls do not get decoded completely, even with their degradation. But a partial cleanse of her matrix and shells from inferior accumulations that had led the planet in an unfavourable direction for her planetary Determinant, takes place.

Every planet is led by its own Teacher according to the program entrusted to him by the Superior Systems of the corresponding planetary Level.

At the present time, a mutual behaviour of Earth and humankind is deemed unsatisfactory by Higher beings, so both of them must review their life positions. Thus, the Hierarchy sends appeals to "rethink" not only to our fifth race, but to the Earth as well. Obviously, these appeals are not in a verbal form, but in one that is understood by her and perceived by her thought processes.

Naturally, everything concerning the planet and characteristics of its behaviour is perceived by a human as nonsense. New concepts are too unusual for him, and this is because only five percent of his intellect is working, and not the fifty that he should have developed and opened up in himself by year two thousand. If we are unable to understand some academic's theory it is not because it [theory] is wrong, but because we did not grow up for it. The same is the case in relation to the Earth.

We can draw a comparison to this case. When a human is degrading [deteriorates], he gets decoded completely, and the matrix cells of his soul are cleansed from accumulated energies. When the planet degrades, only a partial decoding takes place: just the cells that have accumulations unfavourable for Higher beings are cleansed. They get removed.

As accumulations store memories about the processes and situations by which they were collected, the memory of the ways that lead the planet to her degradation will be partially lost once those energies are removed.

However, this will be possible at the end of the planet's program once it finishes. After that, a change of the programs will be effectuated along with a partial reconstruction of all shells [sheaths] of the planet.

A new program will liquidate human dependency on the lower planes. This will be possible due to additional constructions [structures] that will prevent low entities from penetrating a human's world and influencing him negatively.

Low planes will continue influencing only people who want this; those who are avid for various, inferior temptations.

A steady growth of the human consciousness will serve as protection against all inferior. When an individual comes to understand that some processes are low and lead to degradation or the negative System, he will make choices in the opposite direction. This will allow him to rise in his spiritual development and not to depend on the influence of low entities, whether they are in a human form or in the guise of an invisible being.

And this is very important not for the human alone, but for the planes that are situated above him and connected with people by the certain energy dependencies.

A delay in the development of the lower plane and the extension of time for their perfection impacts negatively on the higher [more superior] planes which end up short of energy that results in disruptions in their functioning. Thus, they are interested in accelerating the development of the lower planes within the limits of their programs; however, they cannot interfere with individuals' wishes and the choices made, as that serves to slow down progress.

Acceleration can only be applied to the mechanisms which help to raise human consciousness and spirituality, improve the educational work of people themselves, and the patronage of inferior individuals by superior.

A human must always remember the most important consequence: by delaying his development and the development of a person next to him, he delays the development of God Himself. Thus, everyone has to adopt an understanding of such dependency, and apply all efforts in order to liquidate a possible delinquency of low individuals and to accelerate a common progression of souls on the Earth plane.

IMPROVEMENT OF HIGHER BEINGS' CONNECTION WITH A HUMAN

God speaks:

"The construction of a human unit's network functions points to the dominance of a few accomplished imageries [images] of a corpuscular [particular] kind in a given scenario list, which are located in a dominant position of time-space situational whereabouts.

Actions of this order are relatively equal by an orderly, bounded aspect of speech and visual actions. This relatively obvious predetermination makes the functions of a being [Entity] visible in the configuration of its own creations which, in their turn, are related to the imaginary of the constructive plane.

Planes of this kind provide a distinguishing situation of near-orbital connections and closeness to the highest collapse parameters of positive characteristics. In turn, the collapse of a given constructional layer surpasses all possible constructions of near-orbital structures, implemented by Us, at this given stage of perfecting the Earth plane.

In order to avoid constructions of low frequent ballistic character of implementation, protective disk-like type systems, which provide a defence function for orderly cosmic organizations, are set in motion.

Thus, the decoding of an orbital apparatus, which no Entity can then penetrate inside, is a derivative.

By understanding the constructive imperfection of the Earth plane, We are striving to achieve, in a new round of development, a perfect constructive orbital connection by using experimental constructive settings.

The future of Earth's formation is in perfecting [improving] the constructive structures [constructions], according to their orderly location. In this, the perfecting shall agree with itself; or, in other words, with the body of the same construction at a past scenario of a current plane.

The construction, drawn by Me, is an improved model of the future."

A human, as a construction [structure] and apparatus which is guided from Above, is located on the physical plane. In order to be orientated in this world and to be able to act in situations that are planned out by the program and to connect with other people, a human is equipped with speech, vision, and hearing apparatus.

There are devices in a human's structure which help to perceive the surrounding environment. Vision is the foremost among them that comprehends everything within a certain radius of perception with great accuracy. Hearing and touch provide a very low percentage of information about the world. With just hearing and sound, it is impossible to imagine the surrounding world.

The organs of the vision were built based on the images that exist in the environment. That is, it was necessary to implement existing images into the intellectual [thoughts] apparatus. So in order for these images to be produced by the brain, they needed to be built from a special subtle matter, from corpuscular particles, which create the images "in thoughts" momentarily and disintegrate momentarily as well. This is very useful for the thinking process. With a certain perturbation of the vision apparatus by light particles, a corresponding image creates in the brain.

When a child accumulates enough experience about the world that surrounds him, images can be created "in the brain" even without an initial origin, as some qualitative characteristics (round, green, sour) are enough to be transcribed by the numerical apparatus into a specific image (an apple, a plum). The less characteristics are present, the harder it is for the numerical apparatus to find the correct image.

The received parameters are loaded in the numerical apparatus, and following them, the formation of thought images from corpuscular particles takes place. In people whose thinking [intellect] is well developed; the imagery [imagination] is well developed too. However, it is built based on images that exist in a given world. And through such images, a connection with world and a penetration into the world occurs.

The vision apparatus of each form is tuned only for a partial perception of the world. The insect does not see like an animal, and an animal does not see like a human. Perception is calculated to broaden the world as development progresses. As the soul becomes larger evolutionally, the radius of its world perception becomes larger; and the further it sees the world, and the more its details are revealed.

By means of the organs of vision, touch, and smell, an interaction with the world takes place: mostly, its perception. The speech apparatus allows an individual to express himself, to establish connections at the level of understanding each other, and to arrange actions for common goals.

Besides that, a human interacts with the subtle plane, and particularly with the Determinant. For a connection with the Higher plane, he is equipped with the more complex constructions of a subtle plane. The connection of his material world with the subtle one is provided not through some kind of a vacuum, but through the special constructions of a subtle plane. A human receives impulses sent to him that are decoded into images by a special decoding apparatus which is implemented into a human's subtle structure. However, the work of the decoder is based on the images that a human has accumulated throughout his personal life experience.

A Determinant can only pass information through these images. Any others will not be understood by a human. Thus, "The Laws of the Universe" are difficult [in terms of comprehension] because there is not much imagery in them for a human.

In their world, the Determinants have a different perception and different images, which are completely incomprehensible for humans. Thus, all complexity about the structure of the Higher world and about Their work has to be conveyed using primitive human images. With the same success, we can explain our mutual relationships to cats or fish, using only their images and concepts.

In the same way, it is difficult for Determinants to provide their Superior [advanced] information to humans. Many forms of communication simply do not exist for a human. (For example, the concepts of factories, agriculture, and art do not exist for animals on the plane in which they are living). Thus, there are many complexities in the Higher worlds that do not exist for this given Level of human existence. Therefore, a Determinant uses only the images and concepts that belong to a human.

Based on the influence of the concepts that a human already has, the decoder transforms the impulse received from Above into an image by means of numerical rows and with the help of corpuscular particles. A human, as he would use his inner vision that is formed inside him, or to be exact, in his mental shell [body], sees the image produced by the decoding apparatus, which he [human] extends further using his physical brain. However, the impulse is accepted by the centre-brain or the impulse ring (read a more detailed account of this in the book "The soul and the mysteries of its structure"). The initial processing of an impulse takes place in the subtle constructions of a human.

Prior to the impulse reaching an individual, the impulse has to cross the spaces of two qualitatively different worlds: subtle and physical. These worlds are separated from one another by specific principles, meaning that each world has its own build and volume that are supported by corresponding structures.

In order to cross from one world into another, a connecting construction must change its qualitative base; so that the connection in the subtle world could occur from one type of matter [substance], and in the world of a physical matter, from another. In such way, the connection carries a complex structural form that exists in the different space and time latitudes.

The borderline, where one world is transitioning into another is a separate construction that combines the properties of both adjacent planes [neighbouring worlds]. We mention these constructions in order to dispel a habitual human discussion about signal transmission from one world into another, which is performed faultlessly.

A human usually perceives it in this way: The teacher sends the idea, and the pupil catches it, which is an imagery conception. He cannot imagine the complexities of the structures behind it. Therefore, we mention this briefly. The constructions [structures] of connections are designed for the transformation and coding of the impulse that extends from a Determinant to a human, from the block of energy into an image.

A human perceives the command from a Determinant not in a verbal form, but in the form of an impulse that he decodes further. A Determinant sends the block of information in a form of energy of a specific quality that is transformed by the subtle constructions' network function into numerical rows [numbers], which then further transforms it into images that are perceived by a human as familiar forms or ideas.

Without the decoding of the orbital apparatus, a human would never be able to "hear" what a Determinant demands, or the information He sends.

When a human catches an idea, this means that a Determinant sends him the energy impulse that represents energy of a specific quality. This quality decodes it [the impulse] by means of the numerical operations of the decoder that works, in relation to human time, momentarily, with all the concepts and specific information in the work. The energy of a specific quality can only be decoded into specific knowledge and not just any knowledge.

The imperfection of a human construction has many distortions in his perception of the initial impulse and also many distortions in the decoding of information sent from Above. Thus, a human has lots of false knowledge.

The lower the level of a human's development, the more distortions he will have. Nevertheless, it is not only a human's developmental level, but also the imperfection of the connection between a Determinant and his pupil. The Teacher provides a large volume of information, but because of flaws in the connection, it shrinks to a size of a dot. From the original hundred percent of information usually only five percent is left. The shrinking of volume to a dot is some kind of collapse.

Thus, Superior constructors work continuously to improve the adjacent structural layers between the worlds; in particular, they work on improving the Earth plane's border layer, so there are no barriers for the connection at either side, and so it can serve as the best protection from intrusion by various entities from both sides, which takes place now. Accordingly, undesirable entities penetrate into our world and also exit from it into inappropriate spatial volumes.

Because of consistent experiments from Above, the Celestial designers have managed to improve the orbital connection with humans, and in the next stage of a human development they are intending to use the improved connection model.

Having widespread connections is also an experiment that is helping to improve human construction in the direction of receiving and decoding information with maximum accuracy. Higher beings have contacts with the different developmental Levels; however, these have different structures; thus, Higher beings are trying to improve connections at all Levels of human development.

This will help to control low individuals and prevent [demonic] possessions. The latter happens because sometimes low individuals hear the commands of Entity-parasites better than they hear their Teachers. The link will be improved in such a way that the impulse potential will not disintegrate while descending down, so it will prevail over an Entity's demands.

An analysis of many contemporary contactees by Higher beings has allowed them to make certain conclusions regarding an improvement of the contact connection between the Teacher and the pupil. A human will be able to hear his Teacher better; thus, making fewer mistakes. It is based on the current contacts, precisely, that the relationships between Higher beings and the future sixth race will be built.

THE ZOMBIFICATION OF A HUMAN IS A VIOLATION OF COSMIC LAW

The Hierarch speaks:

"[I am] telling you that for all and in all [everything] there is enough of what is enough in any volume. [Every volume has enough of everything for everyone].

The specialists have achieved the level of a transplant ability of a thought apparatus, which they want to subdue it to their identity. Thus, special projects allow to implement and to be implemented into the psyche of thinking beings and to make a significant rearrangement there, which then distorts the balance of all planned cycle-of-life situations.

There must be an optimal quantity of everything [all] in all [everything].

This is the law. Not abiding by it threatens "the place under the sun" to be lost; thus, exile from a certain official affiliation. Otherwise, a violation of the whole law threatens the existence of life for the growth of nourishing entities.

By saying this, [We] are informing of the disturbance of the psyche in many people and animals. Based on this, the irreversible processes of degradation will take place.

Moreover, the individuals who ennoble themselves to Us and who use Our actions for their corrupt interests are interfering with our work the most. They attempt to rule others, not understanding anything about governing or the results they will get. They want one outcome; yet they receive another. Many mistakes are made by people, and all must be corrected.

We want to warn you to be aware of those who degrade [deteriorate] and who succumb easily to the influence of others because their energy is lost. You can expect anything from them, as their actions do not come from their Determinants, but from the specialists in your laboratories. This is a sort of zombification of people.

Caution at your plane consists in a discreetness with regard to communication with one or the other subject and adopting an alert attitude toward them. To recognize such people at first sight is practically impossible, so it is essential to be careful with all low-level individuals. The candidates for these personalities are people from different regions [districts] and counties, chosen with the help of computer systems.

However, those who are seeking the truth must see what is hidden for those who are trapped in material wealth. Be vigilant and let your heart tell you who is who."

In this text, we are reminded of a world unity that it is not made from random and uncontrolled numbers of subjects and accidental forms. Every created particle and spiritual ones especially are designed for certain goals and participate in building the world, as necessary components. Thus, a human must not treat an existing world as separate and independent, regardless of what it is. Everything, as a whole, forms the unified and holistic world. And everything in this world is planned, and there is nothing that is unnecessary.

Nevertheless, a human suffers from an inflated self-importance. Once he designs something, his false pride rises. He feels as he is capable of anything and that he is allowed everything on Earth. He has separated himself from all and developed into something isolated, growing on its own, but on top of everyone.

Separate individuals, as they advance in comprehending certain knowledge, trespass not only into a physical world, but into those like themselves. Thus, some scientists have developed the psychotropic weapons to subdue the masses to the will of certain individuals. Individuals are being implanted with microchips against their desire and will that influence their behaviour in the desired direction. The program is given to a human with the help of a microchip. In actuality, such a human is transformed into a zombie.

Earth specialists learn to influence the thought apparatuses of other humans, in order to submit them to their will and transform them into robots, which can be controlled from a distance. These specialists have been successful in subduing the will of others, and are happy with their results, without an understanding of what they have done. This would be as if we compelled the kidneys in our body to work by their command and not according to the body needs. A gradual disturbance will begin in a small volume [the kidneys], leading eventually to the death of a whole organism.

By forcing the program they want upon an individual, these specialists cannot imagine that they are interfering with the plans of Higher [Celestial] teachers. They do not know that every human has a program developed by Celestial programmers along with its own development goal, which requires the participation of an individual in specific situations. However, the specialists force different situations on him. Consequently, a whole chain of connections between some people, to which this individual has served as the connecting link, will be ruined, along with other individuals and some other situations.

The events will be distorted. Many people will become confused with life. And the reason for this is that this particular individual did not connect with them at the right time. As a result, a whole subsequent life can be ruined for those whose program included the connection with a zombified individual. Therefore, not only his destiny is ruined, but the destiny of other people connected with him by a program; thus, leading to the distortion of the Higher beings' design.

Violations from one person spread out further and further from the interconnection link, and a whole region can abandon the prearranged plan. To re-establish it all, time and additional resources will be required.

Due to the specialists' plan to zombify large amounts of people in their own interests and to convert them into obedient slaves, they are effectively going against the majority of the plans of Higher beings, destroying them and implementing their own egoistical plans. Besides this, they are changing individual soul's accumulation of energies and interfering with the perfection of the soul that belongs to God. Once made into a zombie, an individual stops in his development.

In order for Higher beings to correct such interference later on, they need to develop new additional programs, as well as additional expenses. Thus, even an insignificant things such as a change in the situations of an experimented person, causes a series of distortions in the Higher beings' work. Naturally, such acts cannot be rewarded. The specialists should know what consequences – invisible to our sight – their actions are causing. For us, the visible consequences are perceptible in the form of catastrophic events on Earth caused by the inconsistency of people's actions, derived from distortions in their programs.

An interference in Celestial plans threatens humans with punishment. Nothing will go unnoticed; and for all violations, depending on the level of damage, a human must pay later and not only with just one life. If the specialists have gone too far in their interference with Higher plans, they are simply removed.

Moreover, the Hierarch warns that many people and animals can suffer distortions in their psyche when a mighty energy potential is sent to Earth, as a weak potential of the soul cannot withstand the mighty potential of new energy. This can cause a non-fulfilment of the programs by many people. Such individuals have not had time to develop the necessary potential in themselves to withstand the might of the descending energies.

Needless to say, this is a human's fault, who, instead of following the path of the perfection, enters onto the path of temptations, which leads him to degradation; thus, the incineration of accumulated in the past energy of the soul. For example, any alcohol intensively destroys spiritual energy, which is why the negative System formulated it (designed and descended it to people as a kind of invention).

If all developing souls could choose what supports their advancement toward God, the result would not be as sorrowful as the present. I have seen as well how many people around me were losing their minds: some temporarily and others permanently. The people, themselves, have put it down to the difficulties of life and habitual destruction. When people who were near us have lost their minds, we and our contacts were blamed for it.

Nonetheless, people do not understand and do not want to understand one simple truth: to seek the reason for all their troubles and misfortunes in themselves. Whose fault is it that you drink and burn up your energy? Some drunks have their energy at zero (we have observed this in the many measurements we took while carrying out our research). Whose fault is it that you commit adultery (in this life and in your past life)? Lots of energy is splashed out during sex, which lowers a human's potential. There is a saying that you must pay for your pleasures. Nevertheless, a human does not understand how expensive it is. He pays with his soul's energy. Whose fault is it that you have always chosen the easy ways or the paths of temptations and did not accumulate what you should?

And now, when Celestial energies have arrived on Earth, a human proves unprepared for their perception [to receive them]. Therefore, the cause of a human's misfortunes is inside himself, and he should blame only himself for what is happening to him. It is also displeasing that he has failed his Higher teachers who invested so much strength and efforts in him. Not only has a human degraded, but he has also destroyed the hopes of the Celestial Originators [Designers]* and Wardens [Guardians]*, who prepare his life program and shape his destiny for him.

The psychic damage suffered by many people will result in an under-fulfilment of many of the tasks delivered to them by the Higher beings; as such, what may happen is that even people who are able to progress, will be compelled to succumb to degradation because of the disturbance of normal connections by mentally deranged individuals. For example, a father has lost his mind; thus, he is unable to obtain the funds for his son's education. Or, due to someone becoming mentally impaired, no connection between one and another person took place; for example, the meeting of a young lady and a young gentleman, who was supposed to become her future husband, never happened and she was left single, because there were no further situations [in her program] that would lead them to meet. Thus, the connections of others are ruined due to one person's error.

Talking of animals that become mentally deranged due to the increased energy sent to Earth, it also testifies to their souls' unpreparedness. Hence, a lesser number of them will be transitioned to the human world. And it must be worked for once again [be repeated and earned again].

In this text, the Hierarch speaks about the insufficiencies of the psyche in earthly forms in general, along with its weakness and unpreparedness for the transition to a different Level.

In physics, if we pass high voltage through a circuit, all the bulbs calculated for lower potential will burn out, and only the higher will endure. Hence, a similar event, such as the descent of energy of high potential to Earth, is a test. The souls that have lost their past accumulations due to the degradative actions and lowered down their potential are burning out [incinerating] under influence of the energy of much more might. Thus, the defects and certain deficiencies in their development are being revealed.

Hierarch, however, continues emphasising at unnatural change of a human behaviour throughout the use of the psychotropic weapons. The ability of the specialists, working in this area to enslave the other and dominate over his psyche, gives them the feeling of self-importance and magnification of own persona. They put themselves at the same level with Higher beings only because they can dominate individuals with a weak soul potential; however, they are unable to foresee either the aftermath of their work, or the aftermath of their work as an influence on the whole of humanity and the planet. Their comprehension of the future does not extend beyond their corrupt personal interests; everything is directed toward collecting and protecting their own material wealth.

The danger of such specialists is that they act through others: through zombies; keeping themselves in the shadows. They manage people-zombies from the comfort of their offices; they place them in front of weapons, they send them into dangerous zones; and they stay unrecognised, unseen and away from danger.

Thus, the Hierarch calls for people to be twice as vigilant; to not trust certain specialists who are hiding their evil under the guise of help, to be careful with one's surroundings as there could be zombies in them. To visually distinguish zombies from regular people is practically impossible. They can be revealed all of a sudden by [with] a change in their behaviour, once an order-command is received by them, and then they cannot be stopped by anything.

Moreover, the large increase in suicide bombers is linked to a zombification. This is an example of how the invention has ended up in hands of the negative System's representatives, who then direct it toward an extermination of other people. This is exactly what I have written about in the chapter "Illusion of Immortality." That is to say, that people's consciousness is not ready to correctly use many unique practices and inventions, developed by advanced earth scientists.

Zombified terrorists do not have any feeling of fear. When it comes to executing their commands, their feelings, will and own comprehension of their surroundings are completely turned off. They are transformed into obedient bio-robots. They are controlled from afar by those who stay safe.

The candidates are not always chosen based on good will. If microchips used to be implemented to modify the program of a human's behaviour, now those chips are not even needed. People with low potential are selected via the computer network, and a special method is used to influence them. The main condition of zombification is the low soul's potential. People from various areas of science and technology can be zombified. While such a future zombie could be well developed intellectually, his spiritual accumulations are so insignificant that he can easily be transformed into a zombie and obedient performer of someone else's will. Thus, it is very important for each individual to accumulate their personal spiritual load which will become their shield and protection from various unwanted invasions.

Also, here I want to touch upon a question about a human's magnification of himself, and about his arrogance and pride. In a previous text, the Hierarch mentioned that many specialists were taking responsibilities upon themselves that were not meant for them to take and learning to subdue others to their will. In a different text, the Higher beings speak about it in this way:

"Some individuals imagined too much about themselves. Precisely this fact served as the necessity to give the additional information to them.

Since the ray directed to the Earth refracts through their consciousness, We did not receive the kind of responding information that We needed. Such individuals refract the ray of knowledge by a magnification of themselves; thus, bringing about an incorrect comprehension of the information and life situations that We require.

This causes generations to be dependent on the mistakes made. It creates an urgency for redirecting such individuals to different technologies to enter into an additional database. However, the database does not accept human intrusions. Also, because there are so many individuals, intrusion attempts occur every second.

We did not count on so many conceited individuals appearing on Earth; therefore, some of the surplus ones have to be transported into a different life form or to have their material bodies destroyed. These are those for whom We do not have time to direct into a new life stage from the beginning.

People allow many mistakes to occur in their behaviour due to ignorance. Pride and conceit are the qualities which must be fought against. Nonetheless, a human does not wish to accept them as vices, and he does not acknowledge them in himself.

That is the reason why many great minds of humankind do not direct their force and knowledge where We want them to. All this is due to the confusion between deviations and norms which affect them and exist in the world that surrounds them.

Many generations follow their misguided thoughts. Nevertheless, We do care about their destiny, and We point out their mistakes. There should be no conceit in a human: he is a small particle. A human is unable to comprehend the nature of the true height of Spirit; his brain is unable to perceive that; thus, his misguidance. In short, everyone must get rid of vice. You must be able to stop at the right time and correct your wrongs [errors]."

The preceding explanation may be easily understood; however, I will clarify further.

People do not pay much attention to a quality of character such as conceit [arrogance, self-pride]; nevertheless, this quality presents a great obstruction for the information channelled from the Determinants [Celestial Teachers]. Thus, it distorts and encourages the advent of distortions and perversions of Higher knowledge. Furthermore, these misrepresentations are learned by the next generations; young people are raised on their base and false concepts; subsequently, these lies and falsehood turn into dogmas. Moreover, when something new arrives, it differs from the old significantly; however, if the information were received correctly, they would not differ so much from one another, but rather be a continuation of one another.

Nonetheless, something different is happening on Earth, wherein the new paves its road with difficulty, through the distorted old theories, which fill people's heads. People have difficulty to abort their old perceptions of the world built on the distorted theories of the authorities. Thus, whole generations grow up on erroneous knowledge.

Conceit, being built on rough energies, closes the channels that link a human to his Determinant. Conceit is a negative energy quality. It blocks the information receiving channels like a landfill that creates distortions in receiving knowledge sent by the Teacher. It is similar to a deaf pupil: he is told one thing; yet he hears another. Defects in the hearing apparatus are the cause. On the subtle plane, this kind of defect appears in the connection channels; but it is the pupil who creates a defect in his hearing apparatus. This individual does not hear his Celestial Teacher and His signals well.

Moreover, ignorance brings distortions with it as well when it intrudes into a human psyche. A human's exaggerated opinion about himself and his own pride promote the accumulation of the wrong qualities from the life situations that a human is given. As a result, a human makes many mistakes, and the soul accumulates low [inferior] energies. Therefore, from the one side, such an individual seems to achieve great success in his development; however, from the other side, recent violations compel Higher beings to send such a soul for special treatment at a cleansing station or a base [site] after the individual's death.

Such a base works at specific cycles and cannot receive these individuals at just any time. The work of cleansing the soul takes a long time. As there are so many of these individuals appearing lately, the majority of souls who are unable to enter at a given intake cycle, have to be decoded. (And this is despite their intellect! The qualities of the soul are valued more highly than an intellect). This fact evidences how qualities such as arrogance and conceit harm the soul.

At the current time, conceit and self-glorification spread as vices among different layers of society. Freedom, given to humans, has become a favourable environment for an inflated self-importance in many people.

Therefore, a human must look soberly into himself and compare himself with those at the Celestial Dwellings. There are many of them out there, no less than the amount of people on Earth. All of them developed to such an extent that a human would need thousands and thousands of years to reach them. Our own knowledge has to be weighed against the knowledge and concepts of a Higher Level, and so one must often ask oneself the question: "What do I know? What am I able to do?"

A human directs his efforts to material wealth, but not to spiritual values. He would rather buy a rug for his wall than an expensive book. Such a choice demonstrates a mistaken diversion of true values. Everything is back-to-front. A human should chase new information and every new idea instead of furniture.

The spiritual delay of humans became obvious, especially nowadays, with the arrival of new knowledge to Earth. A human reads detective stories with delight; however, his brain is so underdeveloped that he is unable to comprehend Higher knowledge. The reason for his lack of understanding is an absence of work on himself. A human absorbs simple, easily digested things. To read a book means to acquire knowledge. Nevertheless, each book is different, and not every book carries the potential of knowledge. Thus, one book is read for a pleasure, while another enriches the soul with high energies. A human must learn to figure it all out for himself.

A human has forgotten the true meaning of life. He works day and night in order to make more money, so he can invest it on something that will decay in fifty or a hundred years from now. However, he must work in order to be able to buy a book or items for creativity, to pay the Teacher who teaches him new knowledge, and to aspire to things that elevate his Spirit.

CHAPTER 7

THE SIGNIFICANCE OF "THE LAWS OF THE UNIVERSE..." AND NEW INFORMATION

The whole Universe is governed by the Laws. Nothing can stay outside of them and out of their control. Those who do not obey the common Laws of the Universe are heading toward self-destruction.

Worlds do not exist on their own; they are created only in order to grow souls of a specific quality in them. The quality dictates the processes and forms of education for the souls. This reflects the major role that education plays in the soul's development in a given direction and also in the development of the worlds themselves. A proper education guides the soul toward higher consciousness faster, which allows for the right goals of one's own progression to be set, as well as those of the world's progression, which brings the entire surroundings into perfection within an optimal time.

There are certain periods in development that are given to humankind, and when they end, the souls' maturity is tested. One such period is the present. Extreme situations are being created that allow what has been accumulated by the soul qualities to be checked.

Any phenomenon of God's appearance on Earth is not about passing a Great handout to the sinners and unworthy, but about changing the human world view. The salvation of a human lies in the changing of his consciousness and the correct understanding of a Higher truth. Thus, God descends to Earth in order to enlighten human intellect, to point at mistakes, and to give new goals.

Here is how the High Hierarchs speak about His coming:

"God descends not to create heaven on Earth, but to get an insight into mistakes."

The bible says that in Second Coming God comes to judge people. Therefore, the people are provided with an imaginary freedom which will reveal all flaws and vice in everyone. When everything is permitted, it does not mean that anything is permissible.

The high moral qualities that high souls have acquired in past incarnations will not permit them to commit immoral deeds even with full freedom.

At the current time, Higher beings, being kind in their hearts, are giving people a last opportunity to reveal themselves either on a positive or negative side. Thus, there are tough situations all around. It is not about the survival of a human, but about the survival of souls.

After the series of tests, some will transition to the Hierarchy of God, some to the Devil, others will continue their development in the sixth race, and approximately another six hundred million human beings will be decoded, meaning that they will be destroyed as individual personalities. One third of the current population will be left on the Earth. I am repeating this over and over again, so this horrific number stays in everyone's memory and prevents them from committing unseemly deeds.

Now, more than ever, when the final weighing scale of every living human on Earth contains all his deeds and aspirations, it is important to give him, like throwing him a lifebelt, the new laws and knowledge. By studying them and with a desire to understand the Higher beings and to get closer to them in deeds and thoughts will allow the soul to accumulate lifesaving points that will help it to withstand the challenges and to end up in the positive Hierarchy, and not in the negative one.

Spirituality means understanding the information of Higher beings and comprehending new cosmic knowledge, as they are the bearers of high potential. All earthly information pertains to low spectrum energy that does not facilitate the transition of souls to the Higher planes [spheres].

A new stage in accumulating positive energies lies in the learning of new knowledge and new information that is presented in the books of high level, modern contactees. First and foremost are "The Laws of the Universe" that carry the mighty potential of High Divine energies in them.

The Laws of the Universe present new knowledge about the methods of the soul's progression and its ascension into higher worlds. They open the path to eternal existence.

The spiritual rebirth of humankind is in learning new laws and in implementing them into the life of the society.

The Code of Laws includes laws such as "The personality law", "The Law of interdependence between the quality characteristics of an individual and his development", "The Law of progression and perfection" and others which are reflecting an individual's development in the whole Universe system in terms of the energy aspect of evolution. All of them promote correct orientation of individuals in the direction of the growth of the Spirit, allowing an understanding of the nature of true soul perfection and the goals needed to attain it.

For the first time, the Common laws of Cosmic development, which are used by all sentient beings in their development not only in the Universe, but in the Macrocosm too, have been revealed to humans; thus, they possess a fundamentality.

Humanity is transitioning to the new level of evolution; therefore, the Older, by intellect, Brothers are joined by younger brothers – people – in obeying the common cosmic laws: global and fundamental.

The moral norms, by which humanity lives, are only a small part reflecting the laws that any Macrocosm society lives by. And we need to comprehend the given common cosmic norms and to make them understandable to everyone living on Earth on the path of progression.

"The Law of love", "The Law of cause and effect", "High consciousness as the law for the regulation of own development" and others call on humans to be responsible for any of their actions and direct individuals toward acquiring the qualities of love and higher consciousness that will help them to transcend into the Higher cosmic community after the end of this current developmental stage.

Earth is given one more chance to ascend to a proper developmental Level. At the current stage, humankind is falling behind in progress; thus, a correct understanding of these laws will allow humankind to accelerate its advance along the path of spiritual perfection and the union with higher ideas.

Laws such as "The Law of the freedom", "The Law of the stimulating effects", "The Law of non-intervention", "The Law of no harm", "The Law of help-system perfection", "The Law of general mobilization" and others have a nationwide significance, as they orientate countries correctly onto organizing normal relationships between themselves not only with regard to internal human connections, but to external relationships too, taking into consideration the common whole cosmic behavioural norms.

The laws include all nuances of development; therefore, they should not be treated lightly and negligently. Even if a human did not grow up to understand them properly, he must make an effort to ascend to their Level and to understand the depth and perspectives that they represent for people. There is a salvation in them for everyone and for the Earth in general.

And let us be worthy of the great goal that we have all been designed for and let us ascend in our thoughts toward an understanding of the Higher goals of development that extend beyond planetary boundaries and unlock the path to an eternal existence.

Hence, let us see the exact meaning of "The Laws of the Universe" (And all other new information presented in our books) for humankind.

The significance of the Laws:

1. The information contained in the book "The Laws of the Universe" reveals a path toward a new spiritual start for the humanity. It removes old dogmas and expands consciousness to the size of cosmic consciousness.

2. Information about the laws raises one's intellectual level and enriches the soul with bright divine energies, as learning [of laws] accumulates higher spectrum energies in the soul which are much higher than previously stored information.

3. The information helps a human understand his true place and meaning in the Universe's System; and mostly important, it reveals the meaning of existence which consists in perfecting the soul and communicating with Higher beings.

4. The information in the book possesses a mighty energy potential that carries completely new types of energies. Thereby, studying the book enriches the soul with new energies and, therefore, with new qualities, promoting the soul's progress.

5. All the texts [in the book] are charged with high energy and have a powerful cleansing effect. At the current time, people's cleansing comes through suffering and illnesses. God offers the true path such as cleansing through comprehending new information and new cosmic concepts.

6. The energy of the texts cleanses the shells from low and filthy energies, harmonises the biological sheath [shell], and revitalizes life processes.

7. Filling up human shells with new energy through comprehending, strengthens their protective functions; as this new energy, having the utmost high potential, supresses and neutralises low energies, on which low microorganisms that cause various illnesses are built.

8. Filling a human's shell with higher quality energy promotes his ascension to a higher spiritual Level not only on Earth, but in the Hierarchy of God; and aids a faster ascension up the Hierarchy's stairway.

9. Timely study of the book will help humankind to transcend to a higher spiritual path, avoiding the cataclysms and threats of Earth's destruction by atomic weapons (the threat of humans destroying themselves).

10. Earning new information and understanding its importance will allow it to pass the exam, which has to be passed after a certain time, successfully. If humankind continues on the same path as

now, the Earth will be destroyed by Higher Forces as a hotbed of evil and aggression. In same way that Phaeton, a planet of the Solar system, was destroyed, which is an example of how Higher beings will do it.

11. Salvation for all humankind and the Earth in general lies in mastering new God given concepts and truths and in restoring and strengthening high morals and ethics based on new knowledge.

12. A comprehension of new Higher knowledge is a path of spiritual perfecting for everyone.

13. Studying the new Laws of the Universe and using them in life is a path to salvation for Earth and for all humankind.

14. Spirituality is a mastering of the new Higher cosmic knowledge that God has sent to humankind at the meeting point of two eras; this represents salvation from decoding [destruction] and the path toward evolution.

We want for a human to be serious toward his life, to become his own critic by analysing all his deeds thoroughly. The legend about God has become a reality. And He will be judging sternly. Any minor miscalculation can throw the scales, and what a human does not pay attention to or what he does not understand can weigh down toward the negative side.

Therefore, we would like to state once more that human enthusiasm shown in low spiritual actions such as chasing pleasures, overindulgence in commodities, aggression, cruelty, deception and evil against each other, encourages a human's energy bodies [shells] to be filled with low, filthy energies which will then make it necessary to cleanse a human by means of suffering and illness during his life, and then enduring the cleansing layers-filters which are quite painful for a human's soul, not to mention an additional cleansing of his shell after his death.

Moreover, the accumulation of low and filthy energies makes it necessary for him to correct the mistakes by which he collected such energies, by means of the law of cause and effect, or karma.

Key to avoiding the mistakes described above is the development of one's intellect, raising one's spiritual level, and building a harmoniously developed and highly conscious individual.

At the changing of epoch, the transition of the Earth and humanity to a new stage of development takes place. However, it is important to underline that this is not the transition of all souls to the Hierarchy of God. There are only 144 thousand who will get there, as the Bible points out; and only those who have achieved the maximum perfection. The rest will be distributed to the places they deserve.

Thus, a human, by his current behaviour, chooses for himself where he will end up further on, and which paths of development he will be able to access afterwards. Therefore, everyone will have to think about it. And though a human can hide something from his own kind, he can hide none of his deeds from Higher beings. Therefore, he must stop in time and realise that he is not going in the right direction. Higher beings are always happy to lend a helping "hand" to everyone who comes to that realisation. Nevertheless, he [the one who realises] must make an effort to learn the new. A human must understand that he cannot reach the top with old knowledge.

THE SIGNIFICANCE OF THE ENERGY DEVELOPMENT THEORY

Why are discoveries made? Why are books written, why is a human constantly searching for the purpose of life? There could be many answers; yet, what is it that he studies for, creates for, searches for, fights for and makes many mistakes for? It is a human learning about himself, about his possibilities; it is his desire to comprehend the root causes of the beginning and the end. And the hidden meaning of seeking a purpose is that while a human is looking for something, he is perfecting himself and his soul.

However, not knowing the processes will prevent him from understanding the energies he is operating through [processes] and which he collects [accumulates] into his own matrix. The Laws and new knowledge that were descended to Earth by Higher beings will allow this to be accomplished. Everything an individual participates in, is connected with work with energies. Based on that, energy development theory reveals a new learning horizon in front of humans. For the first time, it uncovers secrets that were hidden from humanity until this present time. The theory enlightens the world from new perspectives, helping a human to open his eyes to see himself and the Cosmos as a unity, as a holistic process of evolution.

Knowledge of the theory will help everyone who thinks clearly to understand which development Level he belongs to; from where and to where he is headed in the evolutionary chain; how long it will be before his transition to more perfect worlds; and what will move him down or up. It will help him to understand what different energies transform into and to see which energies are accumulating in his shells and whether and where they are more positive or negative. Knowledge will help to goal-orient his own development in the sought-after direction, to accelerate consciously on the path of ascendency to Higher Spheres and to avoid pursuing and searching for an ephemeral happiness and false goods.

At first the energy theory will help by bringing order to the earthy world of humans, and then to the Cosmic world; it will show what develops from what, what is the origin, and what follows. By knowing one stage of development it will be always possible to predict the one that comes after.

The energy development theory is a ray that is pointing at the path of ascendance, as it shines on the concepts of the foundation of the world and the evolution of the Universe; it illuminates the laws of energies transformation: one into another according to the processes indicated earlier.

Its knowledge will enable humanity to find the way of light and kindness, to leave the labyrinth of delusions and the vain search for the meaning of life for many incarnations.

A human became accustomed to having a careless attitude toward his existence and even more toward the existence of Earth and all humankind. He thinks that in relation to them he is so small, [insignificant] that he does not influence anything. And only a study of the processes, in which he participates, from the point of view of energy transformation, will help him to understand what an important role each human plays in the life of the planet and the Hierarchical Systems. This knowledge will elevate a human's significance in his own eyes and will become a salvation for the planet and all who inhabit it.

In one of the contacts, God said that a human "will find out much about himself from Our great position", meaning from the Higher beings' point of view. Needless to say, They think about people quite differently to the way people think about themselves. Usually, a human has an inflated opinion of himself. In connection to this, I will note the conclusions about humans drawn by the Hierarchs:

1. People quickly forget kindness but remember evil for a long time.
2. Life does not make them happy because everywhere there is darkness in souls.
3. They do not know who they are and why they are here.
4. All goods people have created are for the body, nothing is made for the soul.
5. They have no interest in the world that surrounds, as they each have their own.
6. Even when they understand the problems of others, they do not try to fix them.
7. Help from a pure heart is not acknowledged, as there is no advantage in doing so.
8. Every human being lives for himself.
9. If there is the goal, it is achieved even if it costs the lives of the others, which should have no place at the current developmental Level.
10. Their alienation prevents them from penetrating into their consciousness but allows them to withdraw into themselves.

11. Everyone considers themselves superior to everyone else.

12. The worst enemy of a human is his mind, as it is not able to direct him toward goodness and the Higher beings.

13. A lack of faith strands them a million years away from the Higher beings.

14. Living in the present, people do not think about the future.

15. Without knowing the lower [inferior] ones, one cannot say that love is absent among them.

16. Acting according to their consciousness [sensibly] means going against all societal laws.

17. Most of the time a human acts instinctively, like an animal, forgetting his intellect.

18. They have turned sex into a superior concept of love when it is only a pitiful insignificant manifestation of animal passions [instincts].

19. Indifference freezes all their feelings of compassion and love for others.

20. They do not want to understand that the loss of the body does not imply the loss of the spirit.

21. A fear of death makes humans defenceless.

22. Jealousy is the fear of loneliness and the measure of partner parenting.

23. Fear obstructs discovery and bringing the new to life.

24. The concept of having one's own child is considered higher [more important] than the concept of self-worth.

CHAPTER 8

THE INFLUENCE OF THE PLANETS ON HUMAN ENERGY BODIES

Everything in the Universe is interdependent and joined by a unified link, just as the organs of a human body are connected as a whole inside his organism. Therefore, when something in the organs starts to go wrong it influences the condition of the whole body.

A human is just the same in the system of our star, the Sun: if he begins to do unsatisfactory energy work for the Cosmos, then the entire planetary structure Logos suffers from it.

In what way is a human connected energetically with the planets? We won't be talking about the stars influence, as they are a great distance from the Earth; and moreover, they are designed for the different goals; consequently, they have little direct influence on the people of Earth.

A modern human, as a representative of fifth race, from the beginning, was designed in unified interdependence with the planets of the Solar system. Why did all of them take part in his work?

The reason is that the Earth was designed as a provider of perfect souls for the Higher spheres. Each individual would have to perfect himself to such a stage that he would finally be allowed to make the evolutionary leap into the Higher worlds.

On Earth, there are not only the earthly souls. The souls from different worlds are sent here for their final stage of correction work. From here they take off and transition either to eternal existence or to being decoded as waste unable to progress in the hierarchical worlds. Thus, here, on

Earth, hell may be observed in the constant wars and the selfish, worthless, struggle for personal wellbeing.

The thirst for power and material wealth are the main levers that set in motion the war machine. All other reasons are derived from the first two. Were these not also the main reason that five thousand years ago one human fought another and is that not what is fuelling wars now?

If the Earth is a kind of melting pot where, under the pressure of circumstances, human souls crystalize and their characters are formed, then how does this occur?

Let us start by mentioning that each planet of the Solar system is directed to work with a certain range of energy frequencies. For example, Jupiter works in range "A", Saturn is in "B", Venus is in "C" and so on. Naturally, that range is huge in relation to the planet, and the human mind is not able to determine all its components. But for us, it is important to understand the principle of action; therefore, we simplify everything according to the limits of common understanding.

From the very beginning, the solar system was formed to be directed to work for the Earth and its needs. Thus, when the need to form the Earth arose, the project of creating the solar system was worked on simultaneously; consequently a need for an energy carrier, which is the soul, arose as well in the later stages of the Earth's development. First, it was in the form of animal, and then in the form of a human. Everything has been taken into account in the grandiose project at once; nevertheless, this project was implemented into life step by step, in a sequence that is already known to humans.

Humans are of such small value compared with everything else, that it is hard to believe that a huge planetary system was created in interdependency with the work of a human construction [structure], and that humans play a decisive role in this production [system]. But let us make the following analogy. (And even though we have made it before, we are compelled to repeat it; as there is nothing better than a comparison to help understand something).

When a human wants to make an automobile, he builds a huge factory with many floors containing very complex machinery, and he introduces tires, electrical, chemical and paint production. He creates a strong administrative apparatus and hires workers. Accordingly, finance and resources have to be allocated in order for the new automobile to drive off for the first time through the factory gates.

The desire to have an automobile compels him to calculate and create these grandiose projects of the industrial complex and to plan and estimate the return on his investment; thus, in addition to the visible part of the project there is hidden part of work that a regular observer does not see.

It is in the same way the Solar system has been calculated, planned and formed for the purpose of interaction with the soul that passes the developmental stage on Earth. In order for a human to understand [perceive] it, everything was stretched out in time in endlessly long terms.

Therefore, from the start the human was created in interconnection with the planets; nonetheless, at the early stages of primitive human development not all the planets were involved in working with him. They became more involved as his soul was perfecting.

As a human has been orientated toward a connection with the planets right from the start, he has a corresponding inner structure. He could have had only two or three organs and a simple design. However, for some reasons, it was necessary to implement more than ten major organs. And their number is the same as the number of the planets in the Solar system plus the Moon and the Sun. Thus, a human's internal structure is conditioned by the structure of our Solar system, and the structure of the planetary system is conditioned by the goals of soul development (of the Earth and all the beings that are on it). As we are interested in humans in this discussion, we will concentrate our attention on them.

There are as many major organs in a human body as the number of the planets revolving around the Sun. Here should be added the undiscovered planets Proserpina and Vulcan. All other in the structure of a human organism are the connecting links between main organs, which create a unified functioning.

Each organ produces its own energy type, meaning that it works at a certain frequency. The similarity between the organs and planets is that they work at the same frequencies. Every organ corresponds with its own planet. The organ and its planet function in the same energy range; thus, they are connected with one another like two peas in a pod. But even here, the hierarchy of planets and organs is observed.

For example, Saturn and Mercury, at their lower aspect, are connected by same frequencies with the legs and knees. The same planets, in their upper frequency range, promote the production of high energies in a human and are connected with the spleen and lungs. There are always upper and lower margins and the differences associated with them. Any range characterises three stages of human development: low, mid, and upper [high]. Therefore, the same planet can produce low, mid and high frequencies that are particular to a certain range.

The organs of the higher Level (higher in the sense of the energies produced by them, even though the latter condition defines their location in the body in relation to the underlying organs) are connected with the higher Level planets.

All energy, produced by the physical organs and used by them, is of a material type; thus, coarse and unconnected with spiritual energy. And the exchange between organs and planets happens by means of physical energies, and not subtle ones.

Here, clarification is needed. We wrote that the Determinant sends every organ its own energy. However, the planet sends energy as well. Is there a difference between them?

Each organ is a separate unit that works on its own "fuel." The Determinant sends primary energy to jump starts the organ, and it works on it all day. By using this fuel sent [primary energy], the organ recycles [transforms] the energy it receives from a planet.

The organ receives the energy ration from the Determinant once a day. A single fill up while sleeping supports an organ's work throughout the day. The energy exchange with the planet takes place throughout a whole 24-hour day, and it happens only because the organ has primary "fuel "to recycle [transform] this energy.

The planet sends the material energy types to humans; they are perceived by human's chakras that receive the energy while rotating clockwise and release it while rotating counterclockwise. Each chakra* works at a particular frequency; thus, it chooses and perceives only those, in the ocean of frequencies, to which it is attuned.

From the chakra, though energy channels, the energy enters the organs that are in the zone that the chakra serves. Naturally, each chakra works on several frequency ranges as it takes care of several organs and a corresponding part of the body as well.

In everybody, the same organs will produce energy of the same range. In order to be clear we will add: the energy is of the same frequency, of the same energy type. Like a big river that has been gathered from collected raindrops, a large flow of the same energy type has grown from a small spring into a big stream. Why do they gather together and how?

Matter of same type (and therefore energy of the same frequency) has similar qualities and obeys the same laws —even matter that abides by different laws (water, gas and plasma, for instance, all live by different laws) and has different qualities– gravitates toward matter of an identical quality. Thus, water vapour gathers into clouds, and drops of water gather into rivers. Each matter has its own structure and its own laws of existence which promote its performance and collection at the places planned Above.

Interconnection with the planets is complicated. We have to consider the parallel worlds on Earth that have entities that are also connected with the Solar system's planets by related energies, even though they have organs that are different from a human's. The structure of these entities is driven by the needs of their world as they are linked with its functioning.

Naturally, the energy exchange between the planets and all living creatures is very complex. Even in our earthly world it is a grandiose process; not to mention all the rest.

While figuring out the relationships between the planets and humans, it is important to look at the exchange processes particular to the subtle world.

Why are people divided into twelve types according to Zodiac signs?

Every sign expresses a certain personality type with character traits that are confined within specific boundaries and within a set frequency range. But what do character traits have to do with it?

First of all, character traits are emotions that are manifested in certain types of behaviour. Emotions and feelings are nothing more than the energies of various frequencies. Twelve types of people and twelve main qualitative human characteristics work with their corresponding energy types.

On the basis of inner qualities, any individual will produce certain types of energy and send them to the planet with this particular range of frequencies. Thus, a cheerful and upbeat individual produces subtle energy of a certain type by means of his feelings, which he sends to Venus, and a spiteful and sarcastic individual produces subtle energy of a different type which is sent to Saturn. An individual who is busy and fully engaged in social activity will have a constant connection with Jupiter.

Nevertheless, a human consumes the energy of the planets to a greater or lesser degree too, depending on which spectrum of frequencies he is attuned to. Once he receives the energies, he has to transform them by means of certain emotions and to send a new frequency spectrum back. The soul acquires a new quality, which it retains, due to the aforesaid work being done.

The transformation of energy by a bio-energy machine, a human, can get quite confusing as the organs produce energies as well as emotions. How do they differentiate one from another?

The difference is that the organs are connected with a material energy types, and the energies produced as a result of the work of our feelings and emotions are subtle energy types, and they undergo a transformation through the soul sheaths [shells].

Thus, organs work on a coarse energies' spectrum, and feelings work on a subtle one. Both energy types participate in the processes of interchange with the planets. Naturally, the transformation processes of material and subtle energies are different from one another. A human's physical matter is connected with the planet's physical matter, and a human's subtle energy is connected with a planet's subtle energy. That is the difference, and this is the main thing.

The fate of a human is linked with the planets particularly by the interactions of different energies and by interchange processes. However, the soul's life program was developed before a human's birth and takes into consideration his past karma and the new needs of the Cosmos. Karma impacts how an individual will be connected with the planets as well. New programs for every individual are written taking into account these two facts.

Karma provides for life situations and determines which actions an individual can take. The situations are given from Above as circumstances in which soul has to accumulate a certain energy quality. Individual behaviour in these situations will be determined by a person's character and his soul's development level.

The soul's level, or its level of development, is determined by the energies that an individual has accumulated in his past lives. The more times he has been incarnated, the greater his life experience, and his soul will have made more accumulations. Thus, the Level of such a person rises; and in his interchange with the planets he transitions from low frequency energies to high frequency ones.

A human develops his own character, which depends on his soul's accumulations. However, personality character types such as choleric, sanguine, melancholic, and phlegmatic are implemented in a human's program when his soul is descending to Earth. Depending on the new energies accumulated by the soul, the personality type or the work regime of the character is determined from Above. Accordingly, in this way human behaviour is divided qualitatively into the four types identified above (choleric, sanguine, melancholic, and phlegmatic).

These are the lines of human conduct that are supplied by his program, and they do not depend on his internal accumulations. This is not actually a person's character. Implementation of these lines in the program is linked with work of feelings. Precisely these characteristics make a person sad or cheerful, calm or temperamental. If the lines of conduct were to be removed, personality alone would be all that was left, along with many of its qualities already set.

On different planets, there is no pessimism or optimism in Entities; their behaviour is stable [even] and is based on internal qualities that were accumulated.

Sad or cheerful, pessimist or optimist, a person will be all that has been programmed for him prior to birth.

All the above reflects the influence of a few factors on human behaviour. In order for an individual to reveal himself in one way or another, a whole chain of events where situations leading the individual into the certain circumstances that influence feelings, starts to work. These feelings give birth to emotions, depending on that individual's personality type. The same situation that will cause sadness and sickness of heart (appearance of one type of energy of a certain quality) in a pessimist will cause strength of spirit and the desire to fight (energy of a different quality) in an optimist.

Several personality types, such as sanguine, melancholic and so on, determine the individual's conduct; thus, influences the energy that he produces for the Cosmos.

This is a simplified chain reaction in a human's internal mechanism, set in motion by situations. By participating in situations, an individual interacts constantly with his planets, and the energy exchange process takes place.

However, as everything in the Cosmos is built based on automation, in order for the energy exchange between a human and planet to proceed automatically and his program to be controlled by the planets, a human is placed at a certain location at the moment of his birth; so in the very minute he is being born, the energies of his internal program are linked with a planet's energy.

The planets make their mark on the program in a certain way, preserving their power and influence over a human throughout his life. The program's situations are set in motion by resonant vibrations: the energies of the program and of the planet resonate, which serves as a starting moment. Under the influence of this resonance, the increased potential that turns situations on is formed. The choice that an individual makes marks the situation's initiation, as his choice is the work of feelings and thoughts as well; thus, it is the work of specific energies that produce resonance [vibrations].

The planets revolve in the sky and the "buttons" in the programs are turned on, which means that the energies of one or another situations are set in motion, and so the perfecting of soul starts to occur.

A human suffers, loves, and rejoices, and in this way the transformation of energies by him occurs. As the result of this struggle, the soul accumulates new qualities; and the energies produced by a human are sent to the corresponding planets. Everything else has already been quite fully researched by astrologers and does not need to be repeated here.

WHO DO THE ALIENS CONTACT?

Why do the aliens contact people selectively instead of everyone?

Let us find an answer to this question based on knowledge received from Above.

Firstly, the Earth belongs to God, and He is its sovereign. Thus, everything that takes place there must be coordinated with Him. Nevertheless, accidents and actions by hostile space forces do happen.

They have always existed. Our God has four Universes; however, it is possible for the visitors from other Universes to fly here.

The strangers can act according to their own reasons. For example, foreigners may come to our country with only a permit, but they must coordinate with corresponding checkpoints; nevertheless, spies could also be sent to the country, and a country is never entirely protected from invasion by hostile armies.

But let us stop at the scenario in which alien ships fly in, having been granted permission by a corresponding space base and Warden of Earth.

If the initiative for a visit comes from the aliens themselves, and they are seeking to do research, then they coordinate all their actions on Earth with the Superiors at the Hierarchy of God. And after receiving permission from the Hierarchy, they contact the Warden of Earth and solve all questions with him. He determines the areas of research and possibilities, and he coordinates these with his own objectives.

Hence, the majority of the alien ships are here by God's work. There are some physical aliens, along with the inhabitants of subtle worlds, which we cannot see. These are energy Entities, but on various planets they have their own forms of existence.

The planets have their own space frequency and exist in the corresponding energy ranges; thus, all that is created on these planets, all matter and all living beings, exist in the same energy ranges.

Aliens that exist at one frequency range do not see the aliens who exist at another frequency range, as the organs of vision are generally attuned to perceive a strictly specific energy range, usually the one on which everyday life of these Entities is built on. They can only see each other if their vision organs are set to perceive the same energy frequencies, or the borderline worlds. For that reason, some aliens can see their own world and our world, and even some others; however, they are invisible to us. Nevertheless, their own area of perception is broadened to two or three worlds on adjacent Levels. The aliens on higher developmental Levels, which are mostly in the energy form, are able to see all underlying worlds without restriction.

When humans created devices able to perceive ultra-waves and others that could perceive infra-waves, they became certain that besides biological matter there is another kind of matter. Thanks to this the human range of perception has widened; not, however, very significantly – only enough to be certain that what he once thought had an end actually has an infinite expansion, and to find out that his eyes limit his understanding of the world by drawing his attention toward coarse matter only.

Nonetheless, the statements of some materialists, which say they are able to detect any spaceship crossing the Earth's air space with their devices, sound ridiculous. This is self-delusion and an inflated self-regard of their abilities.

Huge spaceships are already exploring the Earth's vast space, and nobody has "pinpointed" them, unless spaceships wanted to be revealed.

The alien ships are covered by a protective field made from energies which the Earth's devices are unable to detect. Some apparatuses exist at the spectrum of frequencies that are not accessible by our technology.

The flying spaceships are constructed from a matter that is different from earthly matter. They can be perceived by our eyes, however, the matter they are made from is completely different, without physical qualities. Consequently, in order to detect it, devices would need to be tuned to completely different parameters than the ones used for physical matter.

For example, in the summer of 1988, the UFO study commission received a fragment of "flying saucer" metal from Siberia. During the study of a scrap of metal it was discovered that it had a biological field and qualities that are intrinsic to live matter only. A hard piece of metal had emanated the biological field. To a human, this fact this is remarkable.

Moreover, a piece has been found of another apparatus that consisted of ninety percent copper and the rest of other elements. A composition which could never have been made on Earth by any means. But mostly important, it was a type of copper structure not known on Earth, which is not crystal, but similar to living cells: spiral and DNA (deoxyribonucleic acid) alike. There are also whole "saucers" that were found, but with no motors or engines on them that could be seen.

One apparatus was emanating biological energy field. Because of this, a theory emerged that these flying apparatuses are controlled by thought and operated using biological energy. There was also a version that they work on psychic energy: this type of energy is inherent only in spiritualized forms. But is it possible to operate a ship by thought?

If the horse is biological robot that obeys human thoughts and commands: "Come on, let's go!" or "Stop!" then why cannot flying objects work on the same principle? They can obey thought as well. Perhaps, the aliens invented an inanimate apparatus that obeys the thought commands and runs on a special fuel type. But this is only one of the matter types on the physical plane that humans have managed to partially research. But how many of types remain beyond the limitations of human knowledge?

There are plenty of aliens on Earth, as we have written in the book "Encounters with the invisibles," both visible and invisible. Nevertheless, humans have not yet learned to identify them and to make contact with them. The aliens usually initiate these contacts first if they deem them useful.

The majority of spaceships perform work that is delegated to them by the Leaders of our planet or by agreement with God. They are helping to rebuild Earth and conduct a range of research. Material aliens [aliens with a physical body] work with physical matter, and aliens in the energy form work with the subtle structures of the Earth and its parallel worlds.

The aliens only take people on board of their ship for specific studies which the Warden of Earth has authorized them to do. He has registered everyone. And if some individuals vanish without a trace inside "flying saucers" this is because of their program. The Warden of Earth and his helpers determine ahead of time which humans can disappear forever from the Earth, whom aliens can take, but must return later.

This explains the fact that aliens are connected with specific humans and for many years they will not leave them in peace. Naturally, if they were carrying out an experiment on a human, he would stay under the observation, and they would visit him periodically to obtain more data.

Medical research usually is conducted by the Medical System of God. There are many cosmic Systems that belong to this Hierarchy. They research organic matter and the cells of plants and animals; they control all changes that occur in living organisms; they study transmutation in every human organ and watching the mutations. The Medical System, precisely, often conducts experiments on humans that are undetectable to them, with the help of energy Entities that are invisible to humans; thus, the System has no concerns about working with experimented-on humans.

One young lady complained to me that she felt as if someone had cut her leg open, had done something to it, and had then sewn it back. Nonetheless, she had not seen anyone. In the morning she discovered a thin red line at the place where she had felt this strange touch, which looked like a healing scar. The pain stayed in her leg for a few days.

Same healing scars began to appear in the other places on her body, but always on her extremities. This indicates a specific field of research: leg and arm muscles.

According to this young lady's revelations, our doctors would have decided that something was wrong with her psyche and that she is predisposed to stigmatism, while the real reason is actually the Medical System's research which has chosen this young lady for its experiments.

Why are some individuals chosen for research? First of all, it is because of their karma. Most likely, they performed similar experiments on live people in their past life. Now the situation has turned in such way that they become the objects of the research and experiments, or are used by energy Entities, who are newcomers to the Medical System, to master professional skills and even by those who are not newcomers but need to gather experience at influencing physical matter from the subtle world and to raise their proficiency.

Many Earth doctors gather professional skills by means of their patients. But at any moment, due to the karmic bond, they can also become, in a different life, an experimental object for doctors from the Medical System.

The Earth has experimental cities where the Medical System studies the causes of some diseases. The research bases usually on study of the diseases that prevail at a specific place. The energy of such a zone corresponds with the energy of Earth, since a specific illness can cleanse a specific type of energy, produced by a human; so that Hierarchical Systems and the Earth can receive cleaner energy at this given place.

Thus, the Medical System, by spreading specific diseases, regulates the interchanging energy processes between Earth and the Cosmos through a human. Or more precisely, between Earth and the hierarchical systems, not exactly the Cosmos. Any energy produced on Earth is captured by those who have created our planet for this purpose. The energy does not drift into the Cosmos purposelessly and neither does it dissipate there like in vacuum. It enters from a particular place and heads toward another place assigned to it.

With regard to verbal contacts with aliens or solely visual ones, special people are selected for them. Any meeting has to pursue a specific goal, such as the affirmation of faith, a giving or receiving of information, the awakening of the human consciousness and so on.

The reason that some people can see a phenomenon, or the Entities of subtle plane and others do not is explained by a difference in their energy structure. It is the same as having a talent. In order for it to be manifested as a brilliant gift, the soul, over a series of previous incarnations must build itself in a certain way and make the corresponding accumulations. In the same way the ability to see and hear the subtle world is revealed only when the soul has worked in specific directions. These abilities are the same as the gifts of drawing, composing poetry and music. Everything needs to be developed. Likewise, an event at which some people see "flying saucers" and others, who are standing nearby, do not, should be treated as a manifestation of talent. One person draws beautifully and another, poorly, one sings entrancingly and another so badly that you wish you had ears plugs.

Everything is explained by the differences in the development of people and by the differences in their structure. At first glance, people are all the same; but in the reality, no two identical people exist on Earth. Even twins that we perceive as absolutely identical physical copies of each other have differences in their subtle structures and in the quality of the souls implanted in them.

Nevertheless, some accumulated qualities are deliberately switched off in a human, so he cannot concentrate on following a different direction in his development and so that previously accumulated qualities do not distract him from a more important goal. Thus, a human might possess such a quality in himself; yet it remains shut off until a certain developmental stage.

Many aliens can see humans' subtle structures; thus, they know who they can contact and who they cannot. Why would they address someone who has not built himself in the required way and who will be always blind and deaf to them? If they see that a human already possesses subtle constructions that will allow him to hear or to see them, they will reveal themselves and enter into contact with him. Nevertheless, if they have certain goals and a human is of interest to them, they, by mastering our concepts, will contact this person telepathically.

Sometimes press release reports about an upcoming landing of a spaceship on Earth. And everybody, for some reason, is waiting precisely for the appearance of material beings. When the time comes; people do not see anybody and are disappointed, despite the fact that the landing happened, but with invisible Entities. A human does not have enough knowledge to accept and understand the information correctly. And even in simple things he makes significant distortions.

As a human cannot see what is happening on a different frequency range, his mistrust toward such reports begins to grow, despite them being true. The reason is to be found in a human himself, in his ability to see one thing and to remain blind to others.

The people who are able to contact with aliens, report that they often tell people: "You do not live right." This is repeated by various aliens, and Higher beings say the same thing. Thus, attention must be paid to this comment. However, despite such remarks, a human continues to live in the same way he has always lived. He stubbornly avoids thinking: why he is living wrong and what is wrong with his life in the eyes of aliens? The reason he does not want to think is because he does not want to abandon his comfortable way of life, his temptations and vice.

However, it would be worth to start thinking seriously why absolutely all, including those who fly from different worlds, are talking about the wrongfulness of our life. Nobody can give a ready answer to it. A human must realize and correct everything himself; otherwise, there will be no improvement and no moving forward.

GLOSSARY

Absolute

1. God, Higher Consciousness;

2. A space volume that represents the live organisms of the Higher Entity, and which contains all Existence [all that exists] and the culmination of a specific developmental cycle.

Absolute [stage]

The highest attainable developmental state, which contains a full set of the required constituents of the energy components.

Atmanic [Atman]

Spiritual [monadic plane].

Causal

The energy that is connected with human actions.

Composite

A set [accumulation] of various energies in the matrix which creates its texture and its qualitative composition [qualities] that determine a person's expressiveness and individuality.

Configurative

A complex form that characterizes the external appearance of the structure which uses few or many simple and varied figures or form types for its construction.

Decoding

Destruction of the soul on a "subtle" plane; annulation of comprehension of "I" as the personality in an individual; disassembly of the subtle energy structures of the soul with a complete cleansing of energy accumulated by the individual in all previous incarnations.

Egregor

A certain volume for containing of something (usually-energy).

| **Energetic [energy] structures** | The constructions on a subtle plane invisible to humans, which are created by Higher Entities. |

Energetics [energy]

A new abbreviation for the word "energy" that contains in itself a more powerful type of energies in its structure for transferring [descending] from Cosmos to Earth.

Energy

1. A new abbreviation for the word "energy" that contains in itself a more powerful type of energy, in terms of structure, used for the transferring [descending] from the Cosmos to Earth;

2. A common measure of various movement forms of matter.

Energy bodies

A human's energy shells [sheaths].

Entity

An intelligent individual belonging to a different world in a form dissimilar to that of a human but having temporary structures adapting entity to the world where it exists.

Entity (being)

An individual [personality] developing in the Hierarchy of God (or the Devil).

Essence

Inner meaning [core] of something.

Fifth race

Name given to humankind set to develop until a given year of 2000 decided by the Above. The name linked with the transitioning of Earth into the fifth orbital.

Hierarchical Level

The world or the plane of existence in the Hierarchy. Levels are arranged according to their order; thus, in a regular sequence of energy development from inferior, closest to Earth, toward superior, closest to God.

Hierarchy

A spatial frame of a "subtle" plane where the worlds of God are inhabited by individuals of a certain developmental level. The worlds (or the planes of existence) are Levels. The extent of their development increases from the base of pyramid to the top where God, who governs all that is below, is located.

Higher [beings]

Individuals [entities] whose development level is higher than that of the Earth plane and who govern Earth and humankind.

Incarnation

Birth of a soul in a material body.

Karma (karmic)

Retribution paid by a human for his positive or negative actions in a past life (good or evil fortune, implemented in a human's life program).

Level

The stage of development of something or someone.

Lower [inferior]

Individuals belonging to the earthly world. A material human's development level always stays below those who are in the Hierarchy, as "subtle" energy is a more advanced [higher] organizational level of matter.

Matrix

A frame base of the soul for accumulation and storage of various energy types which form the base of an individual's character personality. It has a cell structure and the ability to grow cells independently once those that are already there are filled up. The matrix is an independently growing spiritualized structure. The energy filling up in it is determined by God's regular sequence.

Nature [Macrocosm]   A spatial volume that belongs to a huge cosmic organism in which every living thing is contained and develops.

Plane (of existence)   World, plane of existence in a space-time continuum of a specific design [built], a habitat that provides for the existence of specific creatures. The planes of existence are divided by the space or time margins [boundaries], or they are situated in continuums where matter has different energy frequency characteristics.

Reincarnation   Rebirth of the soul.

Sixth race   A new human race beginning hypothetically from a year of 2000. The name is connected with the transitioning of humankind to a sixth orbital that is at a higher developmental level than our fifth race.

Soul progression   The accumulation of energy in the soul's matrix according to a given program.

Soul's power (might)   1. Is the soul's strength consisting of accumulated energy potentials;

2. The ability of the soul to perform all kinds of actions or processes (including thinking); the ability to perform **a set amount of** work in a unit of time.

Subtle (world, construction structure, etc.)   1. All [everything] that is above human perception;

2. All that is created from energy of a much higher potential than physical matter.

Energy quality A uniform [unvaried] energy type.

Thought form An energy substance created as a result of thinking [mental activity].

"Union" An intellectual union of several hierarchical Systems.

Words with several meanings

Determinant (formerly: Celestial Teacher, Spiritual Guide) a higher Entity, leading a human or another creature throughout life, by means of a computer device. They control the program's execution.

Hierarchical System 1. The fellowship of intellectual Entities united by the same developmental Level and residing at the Hierarchy. These systems are located on one or few Levels and have a matching developmental level;

2. A System belonging to the Hierarchy.

Material System The fellowship of intellectual beings implanted in material bodies and possessing a level of development many times more superior than that of a human.

Medical System (med-system) A neutral, independently located Divine Hierarchy that works to heal creatures in the worlds of God and the Devil and is also leading experimental research in the area of medicine.

Negative System A network of Entities that are linked by the accumulation of negative energies in the matrix by means of the processes of calculation.

Originator An Entity higher than a Determinant by an order of magnitude. They constitute the scenario of a future human's life.

Positive System A network of Entities that accumulates positive energies in the matrix by means of the processes of creation.

Warden [Steward] An Entity above a Determinant and an Originator that governs them.

CONTENT

PART 1 5

  CHAPTER 1 5

    APPEAL TO HUMANS 5

    COSMIC (UNIVERSAL) LOVE.................................... 7

    THE ILLUSION OF HUMAN IMMORTALITY 10

    SHOULD A HUMAN PURPOSE BE SEARCHED FOR? 26

  CHAPTER 2 34

    THE ENERGY THEORY OF THE EVOLUTION OF MINERALS AND PLANTS 34

    THE EVOLUTION OF HUMAN'S BIO-MATTER (BIOLOGICAL FORM) 51

    CONFORMITY BETWEEN A HUMAN'S MATERIAL SHELL [BODY] AND THE POTENTIAL OF HIS SOUL.......................... 56

    THE ENERGY ASPECTS OF SOCIETY'S DEVELOPMENT 59

    THE SPECIFICS OF SOUL PERFECTION AT THE TRANSITIONAL PERIOD FROM THE FIFTH TO SIXTH RACE 64

  CHAPTER 3 74

    THE PRINCIPLE OF THE INFLUENCE OF TV PROGRAMS ON HUMANS... 74

    THE SOUL'S FAMILIARIZATION WITH THE PROGRAM OF FUTURE LIFE 79

    THE ROLE OF INFORMATION IN SHELL DEVELOPMENT.... 85

PART 2 96

  CHAPTER 4 96

    DIALOGUES WITH HIGHER BEINGS 96

  CHAPTER 5 122

    THE ACCELERATION OF HUMAN SPIRITUAL DEVELOPMENT 122

  CHAPTER 6 139

    DEGRADATION FROM ASSOCIATION WITH LOWER LEVELS 139

IMPROVEMENT OF HIGHER BEINGS' CONNECTION WITH A HUMAN 147

THE ZOMBIFICATION OF A HUMAN IS A VIOLATION OF COSMIC LAW 153

CHAPTER 7 164

THE SIGNIFICANCE OF "THE LAWS OF THE UNIVERSE..." AND NEW INFORMATION 164

THE SIGNIFICANCE OF THE ENERGY DEVELOPMENT THEORY 170

CHAPTER 8 174

THE INFLUENCE OF THE PLANETS ON HUMAN ENERGY BODIES 174

WHO DO THE ALIENS CONTACT? 182

GLOSSARY 190

CONTENT 196

BIOGRAPHY AND BIBLIOGRAPHY OF AUTHORS 198

BIOGRAPHY AND BIBLIOGRAPHY OF AUTHORS

Larisa Seklítova

Seklitova Larisa Alexandrovna was born in 1972 in Novorossiysk, Russia. She graduated from secondary technical school. From school years, she always has expressed interest for the unknown, unordinary, and mysterious. Together, with her parents Strelnikov, A.I. and Strelnikova, L.L., she took interest in the studying of the ufology, biolocation, bioenergy and learning the foundations of the astrology. Contacts with Higher Consciousness have become the main task of her life. Having stared her practice in the group of enthusiastic researchers, Larisa Alexandrovna has discovered in herself the ability to receive information from Cosmos, after which she has moved into a category of the contactees of a higher level. During the course of many years she has maintained the telepathic contacts with Higher Consciousness and His helpers. She received from Them more than 130 cosmic laws which were transcribed in the book "The Laws of the Universe or the Foundations of the existence of the Divine Hierarchy."

Lyudmila Strelnikova

Strelnikova Ludmila Leonovna was born in 1947 in Volgograd province, Russia. She graduated from high school with honors, and then completed a degree in civil engineering from Rostov university. She worked as civil engineer for many years. Her interest and craving toward the unknown and mysterious have led her into the club of esoteric knowledge where she has studied the ufology, biolocation, astrology and all other "secret sciences". An involvement in such phenomenon as the contacts with Higher Cosmic Consciousness was perceived by her as a touch of marvel. Together with her daughter Seklitova, L.A., they began to work with Cosmic Systems in 1989. On the basis of this work, a large volume of new information, presented in 80 books divided by different series, has been received. Some of these books were translated and published into the various languages of the world.

At the time this book was published in English, about 80 books on the subject of cosmic philosophy had been written and published by its authors, which will be translated into English wherever possible, according to this list:

1. The Series "Beyond the Unknown"

1. Higher Mind reveals the secrets;
2. The soul and the secrets of its structure;
3. Secrets of the Higher worlds;
4. Secret life of the Celestial Teachers;
5. Energy structure of the human and the matter;
6. Encounters with the Invisibles;
7. The creation of forms or the experiments of the Higher Consciousness;
8. Life in someone else's body;
9. Man of the Age of Aquarius;
10. Pearls of the Higher Truths;
11. The dictionary of Cosmic philosophy;
12. Matrix is the basis of the soul;
13. The finger of fate;
14. Earthy and eternal;
15. The Fire of Prometheus or the mystery in our life;
16. The philosophy of Eternity;
17. The philosophy of Absolute;
18. "Personality and eternity;
19. The becoming of Soul or paradoxial philosophy (Volumes 1, 2);
20. New model of the Universe or secrets of the Universe revealed;
21. The Laws of the Universe or the Foundations of existence of the Divine Hierarchy (Volumes 1, 2);
22. Mysteries of the 21st century;
23. Revelations of Space;
24. Conversations about the unknown;
25. The path into unknown;
26. Mysteries of reality;
27. Formula of evolution;
28. Illusory of truth;

29. The goal of the development of a human;

30. Our Armageddon (Volumes 1, 2);

31. The paranormal abilities;

32. The doubles of Earth;

33. The latest information about the development of the soul;

34. Answer to Pythagoras;

35. The evolution of soul: from the scorpio to the pharaoh;

36. The energy secrets of a good marriage;

37. Discoveries without a telescope (Volumes 1, 2);

38. What science is silent about;

39. How not to end up in Hell.

40. The way to Golden race.

2. The series "The magic of perfection"

1. Freedom and inevitability;

2. Karmic lessons of fate;

3. Phenomenon of the soul;

4. The Great transition or the variants of Apocalypse;

5. The causes of sufferings;

6. The optimistic predictions for the 2012 end of the world;

7. Why Earth is changing.

3. Series "Esoterica in aphorisms"

1. Faucets of diamond;

2. Petals of lotus;

3. Star blues;

4. Mirror of the wisdom;

5. Sonata of truth;

6. Ode to eternity;

7. Wisdom in aphorisms;

8. Thorns and roses;

9. Music of life;

10. Philosophy of life (poetry).

4. Series "Encyclopedia of New Age"

Section "Man of gold race"

1. Creation of a man (Vol. 1);
2. Creation of the soul (Vol. 2);
3. Development of the thinking (Vol. 3);
4. Birth. Death. Karma (Vol. 4);
5. Love. Family. Children (Vol. 5);
6. Development of a human (Vol. 6);
7. The soul's choice (Vol. 7);
8. Fate. Destiny or the role of the programs in the development (Vol. 8);
9. The humanity (Vol. 9);
10. An amazing human (Vol. 10);
11. New about religion (Vol. 11).

Section "Earth of gold race"

1. Earth is a thinking planet (Vol. 1);
2. The secrets of time.

Section "The Universe"

1. The Universe and its worlds (Vol.1).

- - -

Larisa Seklitova, Lyudmila Strelnikova

PEARLS OF THE HIGHER TRUTHS

Encounters with the Higher Cosmic Consciousness

ISBN: 978-84-128563-0-9 (Paperback)

ISBN: 978-84-128563-1-6 (EPUB)

Published to print 12.05.2024.
Format: 152 x 229

This publication is intended for persons over 16 years of age.

CosmUnity
Centre of Human Spiritual Development "Golden Race"
Address: Paseo de las Delicias 3, 28045, Madrid (España)
Email : info@gold-race.org
CIF: G13673611
Tel: +34 91 529 6804

Interested readers may, if they wish, contribute in any way they can to the publication of the authors' books in English by funding or directly translating, proofreading and, in general, contributing to the publication of the book of interest to them.

Please send your proposal to info@gold-race.org.